MW00973346

UNTHAWED:
Lessons from a Frozen Lily Pad

Christina M. Eder

Felicity Press

Copyright © 2020 by Christina M. Eder

Cover by Red Paint Spilman

Unless otherwise indicated, Scripture quotations are taken from *The Woman's Study Bible, Second Edition, The New King James Version* (NKJV). Copyright 1982 by Thomas Nelson, Inc. Used by permission. All rights reserved.

Scripture quotations marked "NAB" are taken from the *New American Bible*. Copyright 1970, by the Confraternity of Christian Doctrine; 1986 *Revised New Testament of the New American Bible*; 1991 *Revised Psalms of the New American Bible*. All rights reserved.

Scripture quotations marked "MSG" are taken from *The Message, The Bible in Contemporary*, 1993-2002. Copyright 2002 by Eugene H. Peterson. All rights reserved.

No portion of this book may be reproduced in any form or by any means, including electronic storage and retrieval systems, without the expressed prior written permission of the author.

Eder, Christina M.
UNTHAWED: Lessons from a Frozen Lily Pad
ISBN: 978-1-7346596-0-3

Printed in the U.S.A.
First American edition, June 2020

Other books by Christina M. Eder:

Life's Too Short for Dull Razors, Cheap Pens, and Worn Out Underwear

The FROG Blog: Learning on a Lily Pad

TABLE OF CONTENTS

GUEST CONTRIBUTORS

A FOREWORD WITH A BACKSTORY
(The Underside of a Frozen Lily Pad)

A double dare led me to write a book about what I thought about during distance running. I had it published April 1 as a joke to the person who double dared me to publish the book. The April Fool's Day joke has turned back on me. *Life's Too Short for Dull Razors, Cheap Pens, and Worn Out Underwear* led to the birth of The FROG Blog.

While I wrote the first book, I also wrote essays of 500 words or less that invited readers to explore a different perspective on everyday interactions. I kept the essays in a file until one day I worked up enough courage to hire a web designer. I began sporadically posting those essays on my website and my audience grew.

One frog led to another until two years after starting the FROG Blog, I had a collection of 100 essays. While I was deciding about publishing this collection of essays, I read a statistic in *The New York Times* which found that 81% of Americans felt they had a book in them. I wanted the FROG Blog book to become a literary launching pad for other storytellers who wanted or needed an invitation, home, encouragement, or whatever else was holding them back from writing their story. I wasn't going to let the FROG leap solo, so I rerouted its journey into a collective mission.

Bypassing months of details that turned the tides on the lily pad of life, twenty-three people collaborated to create *The FROG Blog, Learning on a Lily Pad*. I don't think any of us expected the adventure would evolve into a personal-essay series. *UNTHAWED: Lessons from a Frozen Lily Pad* is the second book in what was originally slated to be a "one and done" FROG Blog mission. At printing time, I know there are two more FROG Blog books to be written. If 81% of Americans (and all world travelers) feel they have a book in them, I want the FROG Blog to be a literary birthplace that welcomes readers to see vulnerable courage in action.

UNTHAWED: Lessons from a Frozen Lily Pad leapt from people I met and befriended during a time when I lived in the Midwest and northern parts of the country. Twelve of these people graciously join me to open their warm hearts that unfreeze pieces of their legacy. We write to add value to our children, grand-children, spouses, and others who yearn to witness light in a sometimes dark world.

This book is dedicated to all those who have watched and waded through my frozen ponds of life. You have kept me from dying of hypothermia when my heart could have grown cold. Thank you!

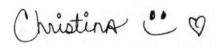

Cold northern blasts he sends that turn the

ponds to lumps of ice.

He freezes over every body of water, and

clothes each pool with a coat of mail.

Sirach 43:21

Teach me how to trust my heart, my mind,

my intuition, my inner knowing, the senses

of my body, the blessings of my spirit.

Teach me to trust these things so that I may

enter my sacred space and love beyond my

fear and thus walk in balance with the

passing of each glorious sun.

Lakota Prayer

UNTHAWED:
Lessons from a Frozen Lily Pad

LETTERS FROM A LILY PAD

*"Answer when I call, my saving God.
In my troubles, you cleared a way; show me
favor, hear my prayer"* (Ps 4:2).

There's no training manual that teaches a proper technique for crying out if somebody is drowning. There's not a prototype that models how to scream if there's an out-of-control vehicle heading full speed at someone. We rely on instinct to use whatever plea will be most effective to get the attention of someone who can help.

In a similar way, when I'm talking with God, if my heart is genuinely seeking Him, my main goal is to reach out to Him. When someone addresses me, I (usually) acknowledge them without first assessing the tone of their voice. If I, in my human limitations, will answer someone who calls my name, how much more faithfully will my Perfect Creator respond? Graciously, He doesn't assess my tone of voice before responding.

God is available every nanosecond and immediately knows my voice simply speaking any of His names (i.e., Jesus, Emmanuel, Savior, Rabbi, Abba). I have sometimes allowed myself to become disconnected from God because I'm worried my prayer format isn't aligned with certain prayer styles I've experienced. Some spiritual teachers have guided me to address God on my knees or in silence. Other influences have suggested repetitive prayer, singing, or reading Scripture.

In a misguided effort to more readily get God's attention by using a 'perfect' communication formula, I refrain from immediately connecting with my Creator. That unwise thinking opens me to a muddle of fears that if I'm praying "wrong," I can't wholeheartedly seek Him until I'm in the "right frame of mind" or in His "preferred prayer posture." These responses only cause me to descend deeper into a non-communicative abyss, smothering my drowning call.

John 10:27 teaches, "My sheep hear My voice, and I know them, and they follow Me." The more continually I remain in God's presence, the more I know His voice (provided I'm listening to understand Him). He doesn't condemn or dismiss me if I'm not aligned with a worldly recommendation that promises to better connect with Him. He teaches me to pray without ceasing.

Perfect Communicator, thank You for the gift of Your Holy Spirit which deciphers my pleas and praises. Remind me I have access to You through the Holy Spirit (Eph. 2:18). Guard me against distancing myself from You out of fear that I'm not speaking Your love language. When I'm drowning in confusion or lacking peace, help me call out from my abyss and know You'll hear and come to my rescue.

From the deep waters of grace,

WORTHY PERSEVERANCE

For the record, I lay a wager to win any dog-lover contest and am fighting mightily against changing today's FROG blog to DOG blog: replacing Fully Rely On God with Depend On God. This reflection shines light from a lesson I learned through my favorite dog.

A parent from a school where I used to work brought a Black Lab puppy to the front office. She requested help in finding homes for a new litter of ten Labs. I saw the dog and knew I'd adopt him and name him James.

The name James means perseverance. James the human wrote my favorite book in the Bible. James the puppy had to be divine intervention. I was distance-running at the time and practicing increased stamina. Labs require much exercise and I needed running endurance. A match made in heaven.

There are thousands of reasons I loved James, and hundreds of ways my heart broke when he died at seven years old. One habit James had was whenever I entered any door, no matter how long I'd been gone, he'd stop what he was doing to search for something to show me. He'd grab any item in his path to display his enthusiasm for my entry. James insisted on bringing tokens of love, including a toy, sock, bone, or occasionally a couch pillow.

One day, James looked panicked while he hunted for a show-and-tell object. The house was spotless, and loose items weren't readily available to retrieve. He ran up and down stairs, whimpering as he darted from room to room as if to say, "Just wait. I promise I'll find a gift to bring."

His quest turned from cute to sad, so I said, "James, just bring me yourself and that will be plenty."

Despite my assurances, he continued living up to his enduring name and persevered until he found a doorstop as my daily prize.

That observation prompted me to understand how God wants me to live. He doesn't require or ask me to make a name for Him. He has already done that (and more) without my assistance. Like James, I mistakenly think I must persevere and produce to get God's attention or approval. Ephesians 1:5 teaches I am adopted as His child.

I often wonder whether God watches me in the same way I observed James as he painstakingly searched to produce a sacrifice. I picture my Creator gently but pointedly telling me, "Christina, just bring me yourself, and that will be plenty."

Lord, thank you for adopting me into Your eternal family. Remind me (often) how You made me complete in Christ and love me unconditionally (Ps. 35:5-6). Help me yearn to show others the love You've relentlessly shown me.

Searching for You with perseverance,

CELEBRATION OF GRATITUDE

I mentor a group of young ladies at a youth organization every Friday afternoon. With five Fridays in November, we are using a gratitude theme for each of our five senses. Last week we focused on the sense of touch; this week we concentrated on smell.

Our mentor sessions include keeping a weekly "treasure chest." Each lady's treasure chest is a binder to collect inspirational cards, compliments, dream ideas, motivational quotes, and an assortment of random items that make her smile. These girls are often in temporary housing, so when they find themselves in transient conditions, their "treasure chest" is simple to pack, uses minimal space, and provides a reminder of support.

During our "sense of gratitude" lessons, we take turns saying what we are thankful for and write each idea in our treasure-chest binder. For example, for TOUCH, the girls' lists included fleece pajamas, Grandma Becky's cheeks, puppy fur, and warm towels from the dryer. They included coconut lotion, popcorn, campfires, and "anything with apples and cinnamon" in their appreciation for smell category.

Many of these young ladies have a competitive nature, so one young woman issued a challenge to her fellow mentees to see who could add the most items to her gratitude list before our next session. One of the less-competitive participants reported even though she didn't "win" this week's most-thankful contest, she was more aware of her sense of touch. She said she never paid attention to touch until last week, when she noticed how soft her fuzzy slippers felt, and the rough texture of a shower loofah against her feet.

I invited the ladies to use our gratitude theme to reflect on one question: "Tomorrow if you *only* received what you expressed thanks for today, what would tomorrow's gifts look like?" I began my list with hot shower water and cold drinking water.

Through these mentoring relationships, I aim to encourage what Paul teaches in Philippians: "Finally, brothers and sisters, whatever is true, whatever is noble, whatever is right, whatever is pure, whatever is lovely, whatever is admirable—if anything is excellent or praiseworthy—think about such things" (Phil: 4:8 NIV). My hope is that through heightened awareness, these ladies (including their mentor) will increase in appreciation.

Lord, thank you for deepening my recognition of the praiseworthy details I often forget. I'm grateful for opportunities to teach Your messages of love and be joyful in all circumstances. Please use my acknowledgment as a form of worship that honors You.

With year-round blessings of turkey, sweet-potato casserole, and pumpkin pie from the lily pad,

Christina

GIVE SO I DON'T REMEMBER

With Thanksgiving being on many people's minds, especially turkeys (the feathered kind, not referring to dinner guests), I recall a teacher's message about generosity. He said he wanted to give so much, so frequently, to so many people, he wouldn't remember all the gifts he gave. *That's* the kind of forgetfulness I'd accept! I find humble generosity appealing and am inspired by the bountiful spirit with which some donors give, often anonymously.

I've been in roles that grant me access to work with behind-the-scenes personnel and benefactors who request not to be identified publicly. Some of the most generous donors can be adamant about remaining incognito about their gifts of time and resources. Like Jesus, who gave everything while He was on earth, some servants positively contribute much and seek nothing.

Jesus teaches in Mathew, "Beware of practicing your righteousness before other people in order to be seen by them, for then you will have no reward from your Father who is in heaven. Thus, when you give to the needy, sound no trumpet before you, as the hypocrites do in the synagogues and in the streets, that they may be praised by others. Truly, I say to you, they have received their reward. But when you give to the needy, do not let your left hand know what your right hand is doing, so that your giving may be in secret. And your Father who sees in secret will reward you" (Mt. 6:1-3 ESV).

I believe, on varying levels, we all long to be recognized or acknowledged by others.

There are days when I proclaim, "Lord, use me completely for Your service!" God sometimes answers my bugle call by offering a humbling assignment. It's my free will to accept or deny His request, but if I bristle after He invites me to an unappealing task (unpleasant, according to me), what is my authentic motivation for completing His mission? Instead of being grateful for God's answering my herald to be unconditionally available for His purposes, I'm challenged to reconsider that perhaps my original intent was to toot my own horn.

Creator of abundant harvest, cultivate me into a year-round bounty of forgetful generosity. Guard me against self-seeking goals that devour pure intentions for serving. Help me understand that whether the world dismisses or notices my deeds, I am known by You. You see every detail of my day. Grow me to trust Your faithfulness even when I don't see the fruit of my labor in this lifetime.

Diving in with countless thanks for Your faithfulness,

Christina

NO SOONER, NO LATER

Sometimes what I think are profound revelations turn out to be merely humorous stumblings, which are more safely exposed on paper. Today's stumbling is brought to you in part by irony, sponsored by the generosity of a reality check (check paid in full)!

It's December as I write this. The intersection of Jesus' birth and the world's killing itself on Christmas preparations is already ironic. We attend candlelight services and step out of the church to discover a tripped circuit breaker caused by holiday-light overload.

I could blow my own fuse box about Christmas commercialism if I light a path down that slippery slope. But back to my stumbling revelation, which originated from a seventeen-year-old's comment when I worked at a high school: She had completed a late night of studying for her ACT test and I wished her well as she entered the classroom.

She turned around and said, "Mrs. Eder, I reached a studying breaking point last night. I finally realized that no matter what score I get on this test, it won't get me into heaven and it won't get me out of heaven."

In the ten years since this insightful student made that observation, I have shared her perspective with others and have used it regularly as my own calming mantra when I slip into a frenzy of activity without traction. This morning, I stepped into a deeper layer of understanding her comment. Though I mostly gravitate toward intense simplicity and use minimalism to organize my priorities, I was allowing the holiday buzz and my year-end deadlines to dance with distress (a dance resembling that of a marionette who responds to someone else pulling the strings).

In looking at all my assignments and appointments, blended with various enjoyable activities, I reminded myself these events will not get me into heaven – or keep me out of heaven. The approach I use to make choices about using my time matters. However, no matter how each day or calendar event is unveiled, I won't get to heaven any quicker or any slower. Some hours seem to evaporate; others seem to last days. Whatever rate time moves according to me, my arrival date and pace is according to my Creator.

The twenty-fifth of December and thirty-first of December are world markers. On my journey toward heaven, God uses different mile markers and speed limits. I sometimes miss His road signs and stumble into life's ditches. I sometimes decorate the potholes of my day with store-bought lighting, fruitcake lies, and impersonating Santa Claus, with promises to bring everything on everybody's wish list. God promises to provide what I wish all year round (Dt. 31:6).

How is my eternal house decorated for Christmas? I pause to realize my life will be brighter if I leave my house decorated all year round!

From a candlelit lily pad,

PAPER BRIDGES

Several times in our marriage Tig and I have hit communicative icy patches that have required additional maintenance to thaw our frigid path. Most of these frosty moments develop from our self-absorbed scorekeeping.

Those play-to-win chess matches lead to becoming each other's stale mate (sometimes I hover between stale and outright moldy). Tig and I are faithful to each other, but we don't always prioritize one another. We allow a simulated form of polygamy to enter our marriage when we over commit to other partnerships.

Pseudo "dates" with new partners may begin in the form of volunteering for additional outreaches, learning a new hobby, following a good idea, or investing in projects that aren't necessarily suited for us. If we don't establish boundaries and curfews with each of these suitors, our well-intentioned visions can cause us to lose sight of our marriage vocation. If we spend more time chasing solo projects than pursuing our promise to each other, interior walls are built, and bridges get burned.

Warning to lactose-sensitive readers: The following includes traces of cheese. I was sorting a folder and came across something I had written to Tig during one of our previous communication disconnects.

Tig, I'd like you to build paper bridges between us again. I loved how you used to leave notes where you knew I'd find them. Your "free" gifts were priceless because you consistently invested in our promise to love each other until death do us part. Those paper bridges connected your handwriting to my heart writing. Love from the woman who appreciates your architectural skills.

Tig has resumed his note-writing habit. Sometimes those paper bridges consist of two-sentence thoughts; other times he'll draw a comical picture, or simply scribble an upcoming event to add to our calendar. Occasionally, if we travel separately, he'll write a few pages about his experiences. Tig shares his heart in multiple ways through handwriting, but I rely on his paper bridges to keep our connection strong. Likewise, he counts on my consistent encouragement to maintain smooth roads for our daily interchanges.

More often than I'm comfortable admitting, I feel tempted to pave a selfish road. Consistently remembering that as a wife I committed to be Tig's helper – even when I may feel slighted – can be steep rocky terrain to navigate. Whatever your vocation is in life, I hope by sharing one of our bridge-building strategies, you will be encouraged to value those people who are most important to you.

Lord, remind me to repeatedly check the strength of my bridges so I may cross life's waterways safely. Help me realize when I'm a bridge, sometimes I'll be walked over. Help me use guardrails when I'm tempted to drive off a road that doesn't lead to Your destination. Keep my focus on the straight and narrow path (Mt. 7:14).

In an a*bridged* version of the FROG blog,

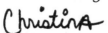

SHOW AND TELL

"Refuse no one the good on which he has a claim when it is in your power to do it for him. Say not to your neighbor, "Go, and come again tomorrow and I will give, when you can give at once" (Prov. 3:27-28).

Author John Maxwell teaches about how the happiest people don't always appear to be the most successful from a worldly viewpoint. Dr. Maxwell observes when success is measured by the *daily* amount of value someone adds to others, overall joy increases (from his message, *How to Have Your Best Year Ever*, January 3, 2019).

Before accepting or declining an invitation to serve others, I factor convenience, sweat equity, and time commitment into the equation. Sometimes, I use spiritual-sounding embellishments, such as, "Thank you for asking. I'll pray about this ministry and let you know." Seeking wise counsel is important. However, it's unwise to lie, make excuses, or over calculate the cost in order to avoid discomfort.

Being a bridge sometimes means being walked all over; but if I want to develop credibility as a Christ follower, I need to be more convincingly active in serving others. Opening today's service door could build tomorrow's bridge, even when an invitation to step into new arenas may be inconvenient or scary.

In my writing business, my schedule includes multiple deadlines, speaking engagements, and occasional author conferences.

Sometimes, without warning, an editor offers me a job I've previously requested. The timing of that job may be inconvenient for me, yet I can't imagine candidly answering the editor, "Thank you for this project contract, but could I get back to you after I think about it?" The editor is asking me to use my writing gifts and resources to supply the publication's current needs.

As a professional Christian in training, every time I'm called to live my values in the way Proverbs 3:27-28 instructs, I serve the world with integrity. Showing surpasses telling. In order to stand up for my beliefs, I need to consistently engage the backbone that strengthens my core character.

Jesus, thank You for faithfully meeting my daily requirements. Thank You for servants who positively respond when I ask for their assistance. As people reach out with requests, encourage me to wisely and willingly meet their needs. If someone else is to meet the need, help me be a person who connect them to the people they are seeking. Open my heart to intentionally listen and look for ways to add value to others.

From a lily pad that supports a servant in training,

Christina

NO SHAME

"Therefore, do not be ashamed of the testimony of our Lord... but share with me in the sufferings for the gospel according to the power of God, who has saved us and called us with a holy calling, not according to our works, but according to His own purpose..." (2 Tim 1:8-9).

I edited a summary for someone who wanted to share a powerful retreat experience. Her editing guidelines indicated she wanted to portray intense spiritual movement without sounding preachy. She explained how she listened to testimonies that overwhelmed her with a feeling that the person became an overnight success and God's best friend. She needed help in developing a "blend of power surge without blowing a circuit breaker."

I related to her respect for temperance. In my first edition of the *FROG Blog* book, I fell short in my responsibility to boldly proclaim the gospel (Eph. 6:19-20). I left out scriptural backing and saw pieces of my writing where I used light humor or a watered-down account of what could have been a more influential message. Like the suffering Paul wrote about in 2 Tim 1:8-9, I was afraid of the potential struggle involved with writing Truth.

When I accepted an assignment to write and speak about praying, that teaching mission increased my mail volume. (If actions speak louder than words, I wonder whether people would vocalize their opinions face to face with the same amplified confidence they use when posting comments online.) Until I see God face to face, I ask for a daily infusion of persistence without wavering.

I believe Paul was referring to worldly reactions as part of the suffering Christians encounter if they live as Jesus did on earth. Some people deny Jesus' existence. Some dismiss the intense need for His unconditional love. Having faith to accept that God, in human form, left heaven to meet us and freely offer Jesus as the Scapegoat for all sins defies logic. As Christ followers, we are instructed not to be ashamed of the gospel and to remain steadfast for the Truth.

Followers of Jesus are commissioned to spread the love He gave first. He made a covenant with us that He would be our God if we would be His people. This covenant is to benefit others, though it's not contingent on unlimited understanding. Through God's covenant, we have been elevated to managerial roles in His Kingdom. We choose to live up to our promotion every time we share the news that Jesus came from heaven to die for our sins, and we are loved and forgiven.

God, thank You for sending Jesus to teach about Your undying love. Please forgive me for the times when I've taken a passive approach to revealing Your power. Continually fill me with the courage to amplify, not pacify, Your Truth.

Leaping with shameless rededication on the lily pad,

Christina

LIGHTWEIGHT OR HEAVYWEIGHT?

"Let no corrupt word proceed out of your mouth, but what is good for necessary edification, that it may impart grace to the hearers" (Eph. 4:29).

When it comes to talking, my word bank sometimes resembles a highly insured financial institution. I'll deposit large sums of ideas and then desire a high-interest rate from others. When my heart is overdrawn, I crave to have someone fully invested in my debt.

Someone taught me the wisest problem solver is one who goes to the Throne before the phone. Sometimes I need counseling, and sometimes I just want to be consoled. Jesus counsels *and* consoles. He has all the time, resources, and power to provide every want and need that aligns with His path for my life.

I'm not suggesting pain should be suppressed or discussed with others when the intent of exposing hurt is for health and safety. Not all topics are joyful and it'd be unrealistic to pretend life works according to our plan if we follow X, Y, and Z.

I used to unleash details about disappointing situations and then conclude the conversation leaving everyone, including me, exhausted. One way I've deciphered whether anything needs to be said during hardship is to picture how others may feel after I speak. If I do need to share a burden, I'm practicing a one-sentence summary to address the battle: "I need peace about our son," or "I need wisdom for an upcoming decision," or "I need to love my husband more selflessly."

Only Jesus can provide perfect peace, wisdom, and unconditional love. A caring individual may be a captive listening audience for my woe, but I pause to consider whether adding particulars will positively energize the person.

Ephesians 4:31 teaches, "Let *all* bitterness, wrath, anger, clamor, and evil speaking be put away from you, with all malice." All means all.

I want everyone to leave conversations feeling more elevated than depleted.

Jesus, thank You for the gift of words. Help me use my voice to edify others. Guard me against unwholesome speech or gossip that can sometimes be masked as a prayer request. Guide me to discuss weighted topics with You first so I am freed to speak lightness into people's life.

With an outpouring of encouraging dialogue around the lily pad,

PEACE BY PEACE

"Be strong and of courage (vs. 6)... Only be strong and very courageous (vs. 7)... Be strong and of good courage; do not be afraid, nor be dismayed, for the Lord your God is with you wherever you go (vs. 9)... Only be strong and of good courage (vs. 18)" Joshua 1:6-18.

Joshua, a biblical faith giant, is told four times within the space of twelve verses to be courageous. I can relate to his need for multiple reminders when I encounter anxiety outbreaks. After much practice with fighting surges of panic, I recently learned anxiety deteriorates me only when I choose to accept an attack. When I forget to protect myself with Truth, I become mentally and emotionally paralyzed.

I searched my concordance for scripture to support today's FROG Blog lesson about worry and found 1¾ page (with a 2-point font) citing fear. The abundant references indicate anxiety has a well-known history. I perpetually need God's teaching about angst (and about all aspects of wholehearted living).

I often use Gn. 26:24 to ground myself when I'm in mid-fret mode. Genesis teaches, "do not fear, for I am with you." I'm gradually learning repetitive struggle only becomes a failure when I choose to fight a battle alone. When God says to be courageous, I believe He refers to a potential physical danger, but also considers our emotional, mental, and spiritual threats.

20

Ironically, God takes my experience with nervousness to teach various groups about how to handle anxiety. Before I speak, I must fervently invite peace to overpower uneasiness. My Creator reassures me of His presence through people, His word, nature, and even a "random" Yogi tea-bag prompt. That well-timed tea-bag message read, "Peace of mind comes piece by piece."

Jesus, thank You for showing us Your perfect example of peace. While on earth, You encountered pressure on many battlefields, yet You remained calm. Release the vise grips of anxiety when I listen to inner chatter before I focus on Your voice. Thank You for Your dedication to help me seek and claim courage.

Strengthening wobbly legs of faith, one muscle at a time, to courageously leap from the lily pad of life,

Christina M. Eder

DEMOLITION BY NEGLECT

"for you tithe mint and dill and cumin and have neglected the weightier matters of the law: justice and mercy and faith. Those you ought to have done, without leaving the others undone" (Mt. 23:23).

In the article "The Friars Next Door," I read about a Franciscan group that is restoring 92-year old St. Moses the Black Church in Detroit, Michigan. They are dedicated to building hope into the bedrock of one of Detroit's most-underserved areas.

The article describes an extensive process of repairing buildings that have been vacant for more than 20 years. The church has fixed plumbing and replaced the roof, and electrical work continues to be an ongoing project. One friar asks people if they would like to pray with him while they wait in line for the food pantry. Friar Alex Kratz, OFM, states, "We say Detroit has suffered demolition by neglect." Toni Cashnelli (2018, December). "The Friars Next Door." *St. Anthony Messenger*, 42-47.

Before reading about this restoration project, I had associated demolition with explosives or intentional deconstruction. In relating this illustration of Detroit's exterior buildings, I pause to inspect the interior structure of myself. When do my actions drive someone's spirit to the ground? How do my destructive words bring someone to their knees?

Those two questions are (painfully) simple to answer as I think about conversations when my speech is like a verbal wrecking ball, or times when I've created communication gaps because I'm building my own platform. Relational erosion typically happens when I answer the loudest call to serve instead of listening or asking for God's direction about how to use His day.

Matthew 23:23 referred to tithing when he wrote, "those you ought to have done." He teaches we are to respect guidelines, but not when justice, mercy, and faith are neglected in order to adhere to manmade laws. I've found when I use justice, mercy, and faith as the roof over my life, earthly laws naturally fall under that covering.

I'm newly motivated to review my building of priorities, paying close attention to weakened foundations. Like "The Friars Next Door," I am encouraged to restore and fill holes with continual love, hope, and care for others. I don't want to suffer or cause demolition by neglect.

God, thank You for Your servants who consistently strive to build communities that represent Your love. Shield me from neglecting matters that are weightier according to You. Remind me, especially when I'm distracted by earthly activity, to focus on caring for people.

Securing my hard hat as I enter life's perpetual construction zone,

A TARNISHED GOLDEN RULE

"Therefore, whatever you want men to do to you, do also to them, for this is the Law and the Prophets" (Mt. 7:12).

Whatever you want people to do to you, do also to them. This scripture is commonly known as The Golden Rule. Gold is frequently associated with value. If gold isn't pure, the product tarnishes. In my life, I see tarnishing consequences when an impure motive leads to self-edifying purposes or indifference.

At first glance of Matthew's gospel, the instruction appears to be a win for everyone. I naïvely interpreted that if I give others the treatment I'd want, they'll return my red-carpet treatment, and we all march happily ever into after-life.

I recall a teacher saying, "Disappointment is a form of selfishness." After bristling from that statement, I learned people generally become disappointed when someone doesn't respond, give, or receive the way they hoped. People can grow irritable when circumstances fall – or don't fall – into a place they expected.

Each of us has a different threshold of resilience when we experience a letdown. The frequency of frustration may indicate the intensity of our selfishness. I understand the weight of my ego whenever I step on the scale of disappointment. When I'm being respectful and generous, it's difficult to remain gracefully untarnished if others aren't following the

Golden Rule (according to self-proclaimed guidelines from the person sitting in my chair).

Nowhere in Matthew 7:12 does it indicate when I love others the way I want to be loved, they will mirror that love. Sometimes people don't respond to my outreach at all. Verse 12 finishes, "for this is the Law and the Prophets." The scripture doesn't offer an alternative-treatment option beyond the law and prophets.

I'm starting to use disappointment as a gauge for my selfishness. Just as I wouldn't want others to place their expected response on me, I'm practicing meeting others where they're at on this earthly mission trip. I'm growing to respect that we're all in a valuable process of learning.

In my humanness, sometimes I think, "If I do this, then they will do that." Jesus taught, through His cross, that He would love me even when I wouldn't love others. He would die so I could live. He would be crucified so I could live resurrected.

Creator, thank You for people who teach me how to selflessly care. Guard me against self-centeredness, especially when I'm feeling disappointed. Rule over my heart so I will love others on earth as it is in heaven. I need your guidance to overrule my selfish laws.

From a lily pad on Golden Pond,

JUST THE FACTS, MA'AM

"Then she ran... and said to them, 'They have taken away the Lord out of the tomb, and we do not know where they have laid Him' " "(John 20:2).

In John's gospel, Mary Magdalene was visiting Jesus' grave early Easter morning when she saw the stone covering His tomb had been rolled away. It was still dark, and the text doesn't indicate anyone was with her, so she hurried to find Simon Peter and John to investigate the alleged crime scene. Mary used the proverbial "they" to assume thieves had stolen Jesus' body. She ran with her first thought to tell Simon Peter and John.

Simon Peter and John acted on Mary's recount and expected to find grave clothes and Jesus' body gone when they arrived at the tomb. Instead, they found neatly gathered clothes and wraps that covered Jesus' face. (I surmise Jesus spoke Mary's love language of service when He folded his laundry before leaving the tomb).

I relate to Mary Magdalene's presumption because of my abundant experience with misconceptions. For example, I see someone speeding and weaving between cars on the road and become agitated that their selfish moves endanger others. Pause. (Christina, look in your own rearview mirror). What did drivers assume about me as I raced down the highway to the emergency vet when our dog had a whole tennis ball lodged in his mouth?

Another example of my first-glance misunderstandings was when I saw a heap of bags and piles of clothing lying near a Goodwill donation center. Thinking some charitable but lazy person couldn't brave the cold long enough to leave their car to walk their contribution to the bin, I resolved to clean up what the proverbial "they" messed up. As I reached the container, I found a woman huddled under that heap of plastic bags. She had a pillowcase filled with clothing that wouldn't protect her from the 20-degree temperatures. I identify with Mary Magdalene's assumed conclusion before collecting more facts. I've seen (and spoken) my reaction before wisely sifting it through a filter of compassion.

Based on a rolled-away stone, Mary Magdalene shared her misguided truth with others. Before factoring her grief, startled observation, and a dark morning when she was alone, she accused "them" of stealing. She exclaimed, "They have taken away the Lord." I would love to hear how Mary, Simon Peter, and John compared stories when daybreak revealed the Truth.

Jesus, thank You for Your light of Truth, especially when my thoughts and actions are dark. In this world of technology, filter my automatic assumptions through Your gate of grace. I'm grateful for Your empty tomb that reminds me that only You know my full story and faithfully love me.

Trading in my grave clothes for white robes to leap onto the lily pad,

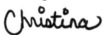

JOB SECURITY

"Therefore do not worry about tomorrow, for tomorrow will worry about its own things" (Mt. 6:34).

Tomorrow will worry about its own things. Ah, tongue-in-cheek reassurance. Matthew's gospel teaches each day assures job security on the worry line. Today's storms are not to steal tomorrow's thunder. I understand how I'm not to borrow tomorrow's troubles. What about when my thoughts bypass *borrowing* upcoming quandaries and I head straight toward *stealing* future concerns?

My study bible notes worry represents division and distraction. Worry and faith cannot simultaneously exist. "Immediately the boy's father exclaimed, 'I do believe; help me overcome my unbelief!'" (Mark 9:24). I've been practicing more single-hearted thinking so I can increase whole-hearted living by starting my morning walks whispering, "Think slow." In the hushed darkness, I repeat those two words slowly until, eventually, that whispered repetition calms me.

As I walk, when my thoughts accelerate and diverge into tangents, I choose one piece of inner dialogue and whisper it. For example, if marriage, work, or parenting concerns overpower a peaceful state, I whisper, "Work project. Think Slow." I find it cathartic to quietly expose the wayward thought so I can declutter my mind.

With consistent effort, I've gradually learned to convert my thinking into praying. If I'm talking, I might as well be talking to God, rather than allow my thoughts to bounce around in my head. God can take my chatter and train me to change slippery worry into grounded action. I'm learning if a thought is big enough to worry about, it's big enough to pray about. Just as I monitor my walking pace to avoid injury, I'm adjusting my thinking pace to decrease inner jarring.

Matthew 6:34 teaches that tomorrow will have its own concerns. God will have new assignments every day, and instructs me to "be anxious for nothing" (Phil. 4:6). Nothing means nothing. I have the freedom to choose worthy over worry. That decision depends on how strongly I seek peace. I am invited to live carefree, full of His care.

Jesus, thank You for speaking to me in whispers. Guide me toward single-hearted thinking today so I can concentrate on whole-hearted living tomorrow. Align my needs with Your wants. You provide peace and clarity when I think slow(er). Help my thoughts follow Your worry-free instructions.

Whispering praises of new understanding from a thoughtful lily pad,

SMALL AUDIENCES, LARGE IMPACT

"Therefore, when you do a charitable deed, do not sound a trumpet before you... Assuredly, I say to you, they have their reward.... that your charitable deed may be in secret, and your Father who sees in secret will Himself reward you openly" (Mt. 6:2, 4).

"And whoever exalts himself will be humbled, and he who humbles himself will be exalted" (Mt. 23:12).

Acknowledgment. Humility. Acknowledged before people. Acknowledged before God. Humbled before people. Humbled before God. I thoughtfully dealt these four cards from my deck of the lily pad.

Matthew 6 and 23 teach about humbly seeking God's hand for all provision. My Creator knows I need food and shelter. He knows I need love. He also knows I desire attention after achieving a goal. When the gospel of Matthew was written, sounding a trumpet may translate to our modern Instagram, tweets, ribbons, and certificates of accomplishment. I value handwritten cards or trip vouchers over trophies and medals (plaque-like awards lead to dusting, hanging, and storing issues for this minimalist).

Whatever recognition method we prefer, I believe people crave an occasional bugle call for accomplishments. God tells us when we receive earthly acknowledgment for deeds, that is our reward. God's prizes are perfectly endless. He always is and will be my captive audience.

The flip side of Matthew's teaching about kudos is that if I humble myself, God will exalt me. What if I was more in tune to welcome God's corrections *before* I misstep or misspeak? When I listen to His guidance, I'm often graciously spared public humility. If I need to be humbled, I'd rather do so in front of my Audience of One than in the company of a large crowd.

Life becomes a two-sided win when I'm more one-sided with God. I'm grateful for smaller-scale humility lessons from the One who is exalted. He can elevate me to places people will not and cannot.

Creator, thank You for Your gift of One. Jesus was limited to One of the Trinity but is unlimited in grace, understanding, and love. Teach me to be fulfilled with Your acknowledgment because only You define my worth. Thank You for Your individualized lessons in meekness to spare me from potentially public humiliation.

Jumping off the lily pad with a full house of new revelation,

Christina

CUT THE THEATRICS!

"Be especially careful when you are trying to be good so that you don't make a performance out of it. It might be good theater, but the God who made you won't be applauding... when you help someone out... just do it quietly and unobtrusively. That is the way your God... working behind the scenes helps you out" (Mt. 6:1-5 The MSG).

My current life lesson revolves around meekness and worldly reward. This learning curve has involved a closer look at my ego. I tend to shy away from public recognition and consider myself noncompetitive, so I've previously dismissed several teachings about ego (although that dismissal should have been an instant red flag to check my pride).

Through Spirit guidance, I'm learning how earthly rewards initially seem prize-worthy. Often, worldly acknowledgment is immediate and tangible. Recognition can be forgotten and, over time, the material prize needs to be insured, cleaned or moved.

Another aspect of ego is humility. Being humbled in front of others is initially agonizing. Eventually, the intensity of shame usually decreases. (Sometimes humiliation has lasting effects that require addressing.) Largely speaking, humbling situations, like rewards, become yesterday's news when the general public redirects their attention or criticism toward something else.

My fickle ego sometimes tells me I'm

worth everything. Other times, I allow my ego's false reasoning to think I'm worth less, even though God reminds me I'm worth everything. At this intersection of everything meets nothing, I need to seek God's direction to clear a path. In Romans 5:1, my Creator tells me I have been justified (acknowledged by Him). In Romans 8:1-2, He assures me I am free from condemnation (criticism from others). That double-edged sword of Truth confronts both sides of my ego.

When I remember to do and say what I would want God to see and hear, I can walk that tightrope of ego with confidence. I am humbly rewarded with gratitude for all God privately teaches me that does *not* get public recognition!

Jesus, thank You for being my Perfect Example of earthly humbleness and heavenly applause. Because I live in finite time, I cannot fathom the magnitude of eternity. Please guide my thoughts to remember that earth is temporary, heaven is forever. Thank You for all I see and *don't* see that You are doing to purify my ego.

Public gratitude for God's reward system. From a humble lily pad,

KNOCKIN' ON HEAVEN'S HEART

"But the Lord said to Samuel, '...do not look at his appearance or his physical stature, because I have refused him. For the Lord does not see as a man sees; for man looks at the outward appearance, but the Lord looks at the heart' " (1 Sam. 16:7).

Tig and I returned to "Apartment Sweet Apartment" living after we raised our son. We were blessed to move into a safe, impeccably maintained apartment in a quiet complex. People ask, "How can you go back to renting after owning homes for so long?" The benefits of renting may exceed my column limit of 500 words.

Our one-sentence answer is that renting is like living at an all-inclusive resort, minus staff-made meals and housekeeping. We really appreciate one monthly price with no hidden costs like HVAC systems, roofs, windows, and plumbing.

By renting, Tig and I have time to take joy rides to observe, rather than repair or maintain, architecture. We're most fascinated by older farmhouses, bungalows, churches, stone homes, and log cabins. We travel to neighborhoods well off the beaten path to be intrigued by the mystery of house history.

We drive until we find a structure that invites us to create an "if these walls could talk" story. We entertain each other by imagining homeowners' conversations and draw lifestyle conclusions based on the house's outward appearance. Without considering what the occupants really live like behind those closed doors, our stories cast judgment.

Like people, our homes represent our hearts. All hearts are in various phases of building. Some are in new construction, remodeling, or overhauling stages. Each heart home needs maintenance for solid growth. Homes, like people, can be judged based on exterior appearances. Only when I listen to the walls of a homeowner's (or renter's) heart can I build upon what others may overlook. In 1 Samuel 16:7, I'm reminded people may look at outward appearances, but God truly sees my heart.

Creator, thank You for knowing every room of my heart. Encourage me to open gates that welcome others. Train me to look beyond stone walls so I do not permit contagious deception to contaminate my soul. I anticipate Your building process to construct accessible entrances into my heart for You!

Diving from surface appearance into depths of soul-searching waters,

PRACTICE INVITES EASE

Disregarding the message that was reported, Jesus said to the synagogue official, "Do not be afraid; just have faith" (Mk. 5:36 NAB).

As soon as Jesus heard the word that was spoken, He said to the ruler of the synagogue, "Do not be afraid; only believe" (Mk. 5:36 NKJV).

In the New American Bible when Mark described Jesus' response to Jairus' daughter's dying, He said, "Do not be afraid; *just* have faith." In the New King James version, Jesus said, "Do not be afraid; *only* believe."

Just. Only. That was easy. This Staples marketing phrase became a hot button to cash in on a growing desire for simpler living. Countless books, videos, and magazines invite our culture to assess their priorities. People have discovered by sometimes minimalizing possessions, they can maximize their definition of quality living.

Some of my friends expressed how much initial effort is required to create simplicity. Their common challenges include a hesitation to purge, concern about missing decluttered items, and the time invested in streamlining assets. I embrace minimalism so I encourage friends to "just" clean a drawer at a time. Or if they "only" organize a closet for five minutes every day, they will be closer to their lighten-the-load goal.

My use of "just" and "only" words may inadvertently minimize a struggle people face when releasing their possessions. But "just" because I've adopted extreme simplicity doesn't help push another person's "that was easy" button (In fact, in some cases my "only" solutions may push hot buttons).

As the Creator of the universe, Jesus in human form came to earth equipped with faith. I wonder if the synagogue official heard "only" and "just" in the amplified way my friends hear my simplification process. In the middle of my current struggle, reading "just" and "only" have helped me realize whether I'm building faith or lessening earthly priorities; consistent practice is essential to develop strength.

Jesus, help me have faith only in You, the just God of the universe. I live in a culture that markets ease and comfort. Guide me to recognize strength and courage are not built by the touch of a button. Continue teaching me to develop more skills instead of wishing for fewer problems. Thank You for reminding me to fear not, to "just" have faith!

With growing ease and trust through practice,

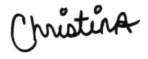

SIGNS IN THE SKY

"Fire and hail, snow and clouds; Stormy wind, fulfilling His word" (Ps. 148:8).

According to Psalms 148, fire, hail, snow, clouds, and winds are fulfilling God's word. Each weather condition is simply doing what God created it to do. When it comes to conversational icebreakers, weather receives a lot of air time. Climate conditions sometimes open storm-shelter discussions for even the most potentially disastrous encounters.

As a world, we are experiencing atypical precipitation and temperature patterns in areas that don't ordinarily see ice, snow, and flooding. Beyond howling winds, thunder, or pelting hail, weather noise is relatively quiet. However, the once-quiet weather conditions speak volumes when discussing aftermaths of ice, flooding, snow, and fire.

I'm fascinated by how our Creator uses a neutral universal experience to unite His world. Nobody is exempt from being affected by nature to some degree. God uses weather and its effects to grab everyone's attention and invite us to step away from our sometimes climate-controlled environment and work in different ways. He celebrates diversity by unifying our survival needs. The weather becomes a common denominator in which everyone is factored into His equation.

We throw caution to the wind when we strive to control many areas of our lives. Weather is controlled only by the One who created all. People refer to weather upsets as an Act of God. I'm grateful credit is given where credit is due.

We're surprised by hurricanes, earthquakes, and tornados. Insurance companies categorize Acts of God, but I don't believe God is simply acting. He's acting with purpose. He isn't shocked because these *are* natural (to Him) disasters. Climate can teach us to adjust our Doppler radar to depend on our Perfect Chief Meteorologist.

Much has been discussed about end times and seeing external signs. A sky check isn't necessarily required because God crafted a signal in our DNA if we are willing to discover it. With regular surveillance, our Spirit-led conscience allows us to detect much of what may be overlooked in the whirlwinds of life.

Creator of all, Thank You for the gift of changing weather patterns. Shifting winds encourage me to be aware of Your power and energy. Make me fireproof. Guard my heart against becoming icy or snowed under by acts that are not planned on Your Radar.

Seeking His reign accumulation to flood my heart, especially when I'm weathering a storm on my lily pad,

CHEW ON THIS

"But now we are famished; we see noth-ing before us but this manna" (Num. 11:6).

After reading Numbers 11, I visualize a biblical interpretation of the children's story, *If You Give a Mouse a Cookie*. In her endearing book, author Laura Numeroff writes about a mouse who wants a cookie. When someone gives him a cookie, then he'll ask for a glass of milk, then a straw, then a napkin, and the list continues until the mouse returns full circle to ask for another cookie.

Numbers 11:6 tells how the Israelites were famished, yet they complained about manna. Moses faced approximately 600,000 irritable "mice" yearning for what they had in Egypt. The Israelites whined for what they thought they wanted in the Promised Land. They focused on their famine rather than their sky-delivered feast. By the end of their forty-year wandering pilgrimage, I wonder whether Moses thought his mice had grown into rats!

I'm like that mouse story's character when I want earthly life to satisfy me. Yes, sometimes I *do* want a cookie, but more often, my cravings aren't pacified with a simple cookie. My wanna-be mouse story might read, "If you give Christina a book, then she'll immediately want time to read it, then she'll want a mug of coffee, then she'll want a warm blanket, then she'll want a quiet space, then..."

How often do I see the gaps between my

needs and wants instead of noticing what has already been filled? When do I become like an ungrateful Israelite who bellyached for meat? In their childish state, how would the Israelites be able to chew meat from animals when they wouldn't even nibble bread from heaven?

I like to think Moses might have had more compassion for the Israelites if they had appreciated their "is" more than their "was" or what "will hopefully be."

Provider of all, I thank You for Your minute-by-minute provision. Train me to see more of Your supply and less of my demand. Thank You for your ever-present faithfulness to uphold my trust for future loyalty.

From a fully supplied, wander-less lily pad,

FRESHLY SUNBURNT

"That which has been is what will be, that which is done is what will be done, and there is nothing new under the sun. Is there anything of which it may be said, 'See this is new'?" (Eccl. 1:9-10)

"Through the Lord's mercies we are not consumed, Because His compassions fail not. They are new every morning; Great is Your faithfulness" (Lam. 3:22-23).

I remember reading "nothing new under the sun" from Ecclesiastes when I was in my late 20s. My reaction was, "Well, if nothing is new, why should I bother, and what is the reason for my being on this earthly mission?" I questioned how Ecclesiastes 1:9 taught about nothing new under the sun and Lamentations 3:22-23 wrote of how God's mercies are new every morning. I allowed my misguided connection between these two scriptures to confuse and frustrate me.

Thinking is good. But overthinking can become despairing. Since that first read from Ecclesiastes, I've traveled more than twenty revolutions around the sun. My additional time travel has shined a beam of enlightened understanding.

I'm reassured by Lamentations' teaching that God mercifully grants a new chance for me to shine every morning. Each day I get to wake to the mercy that has been restocked and freshly brewed. That mercy for me *is* something new under the sun!

Ecclesiastes invites hope because "nothing new under the sun" also means God is not shocked or concerned when something new-to-me creates havoc. He has a solution before I even realize I have a problem.

I appreciate these lessons, especially as I work toward my first anthology deadline. I'm finding out how much I need others to teach me their "nothing new (to them) under the sun" knowledge. I require much assistance from seasoned editors, publishers, technologists, illustrators, accountants, and writers. These professionals became professional because they learned from someone else who learned from someone else who...

These people's nothing-new-under-the-sun expertise has been crucial. I try to fathom this publishing process without light from these business stars. We live in an odd little world where we desire courageous innovation and we simultaneously want comfortable security. I *say* there's no reason to reinvent the wheel, yet *live* to explore under an eclipse of moderately known conditions.

Sun Maker and Mercy Giver, Thank You for Your light of hope. Help me cast out the shadows of doubt when the path ahead of me appears unlit. Guard me against hazy thinking. Thank You for guidance from those generous people who share their skills learned from others.

Reveling in both new mercies and fresh sunlight from the lily pad,

Christina

WEIGHT OFF MY SHOULDERS

"I will come down and speak with you there. I will also take some of the spirit that is on you and will bestow it on them, that they may share the burden of the people with you. You will then not have to bear it by your-self" (Num. 11:17).

In Numbers, the Lord met Moses at the intersection of famished and fed up.

Moses is in the desert, exhausted from leading an estimated 2.4 million murmuring Israelites filling him with hot air pressure. God extends His mercy and graciously supplies 70 elders and authorities for Moses' trip to the Promised Land.

Numbers 11:17 displays a trifecta of God's love. First, He comes from heaven to minister to Moses. I try to picture God stopping by my *Martha and Mary Writing Studio*. How would I react if He knocked on my office door to help write today's FROG Blog?

Second, the Lord transfers some of Moses' spirit onto 70 faithful authorities. The text doesn't specify if this spiritual transaction referred to Moses' weakened spirit or to his spirit of anointed leadership. The crux is that some pressure was lifted from Moses.

Third, by receiving part of Moses' spirit, 70 elders were promoted to co-manage a God-ordained task force. The elders' commissioning package included approximately 2.4 million naysayers who were impatient to reach the Promised Land. The Numbers passage doesn't indicate whether those 70 authorities were part of the grumbling crew prior to being called to assist the understaffed Moses.

In my walk toward the eternal Promised Land, I have served on Team Moses through teaching and leading roles. I admit I've been involved with Team Israelite and "shared" my prickly witness. Like God did with Moses, He has been faithful to send people who shoulder my burden (and knock the burden chip off my shoulder). God's physical presence appears through compassionate people sharing His generous love.

Jesus, thank You for showcasing Your presence through others. I'm grateful for wise mentors and elders who guide me toward You. Guard me against murmuring and complaining. Protect me from wilderness wandering so I can finish Your earthly mission with graceful testimony.

From an elevated lily pad,

PIGS AND PEARLS

"... heaven is like a merchant seeking beautiful pearls, who, when he had found one pearl of great price, went and sold all that he had and bought it" (Mt. 13:45-46).

"... nor cast your pearls before swine, lest they trample them under their feet, and turn and tear you in pieces" (Mt. 7:6).

Before my daily quiet time, I walk outside for fresh air and mentally purge. This "brain dump" allows me to clear my mind so I can better hear God. My patchwork of thoughts doesn't necessarily follow any pattern. I simply whisper my concerns, joys, musings, and dreams as I walk.

Lately, my morning quiet times have been so intense I need to do a short power walk afterward to release an energy surge. I learned this post-quiet time walking strategy the hard way. Instead of first digesting God's insight before speaking, I quickly dialed a close friend to divulge a 7½-minute spiritual revelation at food-processor speed.

Bypassing harsh conversational details from that unprepared recipient, I discovered that sometimes what happens in quiet time needs to stay in quiet time. In Mt. 13:45, I learn seeking heaven is like seeking pearls. And Mt. 7:6 reminds me I am not to cast those pearls before swine. (In no way am I comparing my unsuspecting phone-call recipient to swine.)

When God's insights are so rich, I yearn to shout them to anyone and everyone. My Creator piggybacks teaching moments so I can also practice tempered discernment. Just because He introduces me to larger-picture thinking doesn't mean the world is ready to deep-sea dive into salty waters with me. God will prepare messengers to help me cultivate and deliver pearls of wisdom.

This morning, after yet another powerful quiet time, I headed outside for a decompressing walk. I looked down at my feet and saw a white-painted bead, most likely from a child's broken necklace. That scratched plastic bead may have once been a cheap adornment, but today it served as my priceless reminder. I am to continue seeking heaven's wisdom and also be cautious about casting pearls to swine.

Creator, thank You for imparting me with pearls of wisdom. String discernment around my neck so I may better know when to clasp Your word in the silence of my heart. Guard me against flooding people when they are not yet ready to receive Your genuine pearls. And thank You for Your fresh-water guidance when I attempt to dive into the salt-water territory.

Seeking more pearls of wisdom from the lily pad,

EFFICIENT WORD COUNT

"And Jesus answered and said to him, 'Simon, I have something to say to you.' So he said, 'Teacher, say it' " (Luke 7:40).

Jesus, as Teacher, asking His student's permission to speak? Since when did this hierarchy between student and teacher shift?

Jesus was at a celebration hosted by a man named Simon. A woman, only defined as a "sinner," also attended this social. I presume she wasn't on Simon's guest list, but nonetheless, he continued his hosting duties until she suddenly broke a jar of expensive perfume over Jesus' head and threw herself at His feet.

This nameless woman wept and washed Jesus' feet with her fragrant oil and tears. Simon probably knew oil and water didn't mix, but instead of cleaning up the mess, he made a clean-sweep judgment. In one efficient sentence, Simon challenged Jesus' discernment and the woman's behavior. Luke 7:39 writes, "... if He were a prophet, He would know who and what manner of woman this is who is touching Him, for she is a sinner" (NKJV).

Simon called Jesus out in front of his party crowd. Jesus' male ego didn't defensively retaliate. He graciously recognized Simon as the host of this house party and respectfully told Simon He had something to say to him. Instead of using His authority to lord over him, Jesus waited for Simon's go-ahead before He spoke.

The ironic plot thickened. Simon, in his

verbal efficiency, acknowledged and snubbed Jesus in a three-word response: "Teacher, say it." Simon honored Jesus' anointed position as Teacher, yet when he told Jesus to say it, I sense reluctant yielding. I "hear" Simon's tone as if to imply, "Yeah, yeah, yeah, Jesus, get on with it already. I'm listening."

I visualize fellow partygoers stopping mid-bite or dropping dinnerware to watch Jesus' next move. I wonder if they were surprised at Jesus' steadfast peace in telling Simon a forgiveness story between a creditor and debtor.

In one simple verse, I learned how Jesus respected the house and its owner. He gently responded to an atypical situation, patiently teaching Simon about guest hospitality and forgiveness. Jesus won the ultimate party game by practicing what He preached when He lovingly absolved the repentant woman of her sins. I'm no seasoned partygoer, but I've never seen a bouncer respond to a party crowd as Jesus did at Simon's house. He verbally escorted her to the door with His parting gift, "Go in peace."

Jesus, thank You for Your effective teaching through few words and many actions. When I'm challenged, defend me against disrespect. Guide me to persistently respond with peaceful Truth. Thank You for Your gift of forgiveness and seeing what's best for me, even when I'm showing up at my worst.

Breaking my alabaster jar over the lily pad and leaping from fragrantly oiled leaves,

WIDOWS OPENED WINDOWS

"... to visit orphans and widows in their trouble, and to keep oneself unspotted from the world" (James 1:27).

Three widowers. One marriage. I had the honor of hearing three people at various phases of the grieving journey share stories about their deceased spouses. These two women and one man unknowingly served as marriage mentors for me during a week when my own marital vows were being particularly tested.

They opened wounded hearts to reveal memories about projects they tackled together, and dreams they wouldn't fulfill with each other. Each path was drastically different, yet a sense of deep loss united these grieving spouses' journeys. While they talked about times when "heated words of intense fellowship" occurred, all three people insisted they'd relive those temporary lapses of harmony versus living without their spouse.

James 1:27 instructs us to visit orphans and widows in their troubles. Through these widows' trust and willingness to allow me to visit, I received incredible insight about grieving. I learned how important it is to guard my tongue when my husband is angry. I found out how smiles and hand-holding became cherished reminders of the missing spouse.

I heard a once-insignificant item – like a coffee mug or a sweater – increases in value when the spouse is not there to use it. I also discovered how painful it is to comfort a pet while he searches the house for his other master. I also found out how stressful car maintenance, insurance dealings, and meals become when a partnership shifts to a sole responsibility.

Acts 6:1 discusses how the church cares for the widows. These three people, by imparting their marital wisdom through loss, cared for me! I followed James' teaching to visit the widows. The second half of that verse reads, "to keep oneself unspotted from the world." I believe, through the generous revelations of these grieving spouses, I am better equipped to strive to keep my marriage (nearly) unspotted.

Jesus, thank You for the invitation to visit widows and orphans. From this surprise connection during a marital disconnection, I gained priceless lessons. Guard me against petty disagreements that would pale behind a shadow of death. Light the paths for all widows and orphans walking without their loved ones' earthly presence. Thank You for Your promise of eternity as You prepare a place for all believers to reunite without any suffering.

Leaping from a lily pad to walk the bridge between earth and heaven,

Christina

AS THE WORLD TURNS AND AS THE WORLD GOES AWAY

"But now I come to You, and these things I speak in the world... I have given them Your word; and the world hated them because they are not of the world, just as I am not of the world" (John 17:13-14).

I appreciate how Jesus recognized He didn't fit into the world. He had His haters, scoffers, and eye rollers; yet He didn't allow unbelievers to diminish His confidence in the earthly mission for which God sent Him. Jesus didn't have a layer of internet protection to electronically shield Him from any in-His-face opinions, either!

Pastors and other ministers of the Word can relate to Jesus in knowing they've been called to teach God's love and people openly shun or dismiss His message. When a Christ follower lives Truth, he or she may encounter some of the animosity Jesus experienced. We believers can become targets for verbal and physical attacks when bitterness is shot from barrels of uninformed or misguided assumptions.

Jesus knew His earthly purpose was to bring heavenly devotion to a world that desperately needs love. The world represents people who oppose God's love. Unrestricted love isn't logical or practical today, nor did it make sense when Jesus was on earth; so misguided haters crucified Love. On Good Friday, the world thought executioners succeeded in killing Truth, but Love rose to the occasion and shined resurrected Light. Jesus, as Love and Truth, wouldn't and couldn't allow death to have the last word.

I hurt when people don't "get me" or disagree with how I live out God's love. When I read John 17:13-14, I remember how Jesus rolled away a rock of misunderstanding. So instead of downplaying Truth or witnessing louder, I remind myself Who has the final say about me. God's eternal Word will last after I pass through this temporary world.

Creator, thank You for sending Jesus to show Perfect Love to an imperfect world. When I'm distracted by how I'm viewed by (what seems to be) a world majority, anchor me to The Minority who fully understands. Thank You for warming our world with Your perpetual light!

Using FROG legs to serve from an out-of-this-world lily pad,

Christina

FASTING HEART RATE

"Why do we fast, and you do not see it?
Afflict ourselves, and you take no note of it?"
(Is. 58:3 NAB).

Yesterday I wrote from Isaiah 57:1, using the example of an upright man's death going seemingly unnoticed. Today, in Isaiah 58:3, the people cry out for God's attention. They are starving and wondering why God isn't applauding their fasting efforts. From man's lack of recognition to craving God's attention, a foiled pattern of disregard is woven into these back-to-back chapters.

Further into Isaiah 58, we learn God is not impressed with their fast because, although they refrain from food, they indulge in argument and fighting. God doesn't instruct us to fast simply to cause hunger pangs. He wants us to use that sacrificial discomfort to signal awareness to fill others' needs. My empty stomach is to represent a gap only my Creator can fill.

God and I are the only ones who should know about the discomfort associated with fasting (Mt. 6:16-18). He calls followers to fast *and pray* in private and to serve in public. My motive and actions, in conjunction with fasting, gain God's attention and movement to prayers. He looks at my heart. If I'm faithfully using my life to share God's love with others, He recognizes every effort. When my heart beats to help God's world, it becomes the rhythm of my soul.

Jesus, thank You for showing me Your heart. Match my motives to lighten people's burdens. When You call me to fast, guard me against irritability and complaining. Please use my absence of food to feed the needs of a hurting world. Thank You that my sacrificial fast doesn't include the Cross, which Jesus endured for me.

Heartfully grateful from the lily pad,

ADJUST THE FREQUENCY

"O God, You are my God; Early will I seek You; my soul thirsts for You; My flesh longs for You In a dry and thirsty land where there is no water" (Ps. 63:1).

"It is good that one should hope and wait quietly for the salvation of the Lord" (Lam. 3:26).

When I worked in the cubicle world, I had a distorted concept of what it would be like to be a career author and public speaker. Now I work from the *Martha and Mary Writing Studio* and when people ask about my writer's life, I answer, "Most days it's like Lucille Ball meets Roma Downey in *Touched by an Angel.*"

Like Martha in Luke's gospel (Lk. 10:38-42), Lucille Ball from *I Love Lucy* tries to serve and solve from a well-meaning heart. Through their perpetual motion, these characters may relate to the psalmist, seeking assistance with seemingly little understanding.

Some days I feverishly write pages of content, only to salvage one puny paragraph that warrants value. Like the psalmist, I begin my day giving credit to my Creator. I seek, thirst, and long for God even in a dry land where there is no water. Sometimes my written brainstorms turn out to be no more than a drizzle, yet I know God is present and desires to be sought, especially in arid conditions.

Comparatively speaking, Martha's sister Mary and Monica (Roma Downey) await Divine

Revelation. Both remain gently hopeful until they become aware of the Holy Spirit's arrival.

Through faithful placement of a glowing light, the producers of *Touched by an Angel* trained viewers to expect that yellowish hue on the screen when Monica's angelic presence is made known. That glow only appears at the end of each episode, yet viewers anticipate it.

God's show has a longer running history than either *I Love Lucy* or *Touched by an Angel* and He's produced endless episodes of trust to remind us His Light will shine. Today, I tune the FROG Blog channel to Psalm 63:1 and Lamentations 3:26 to await His broadcast.

Psalms 63:1 teaches me the consistent practice of faith. In learning, writing, and teaching about God, I find a continuous blend between striving and surrendering; between accelerating and coasting.

Lamentations 3:26 quenches the psalmist's thirst for God. Not only is it good to wait quietly, but with the anticipation that God *will* make His presence known. The caveat to God's promises is *when* they will be revealed. We are to remain watchful until God unveils each promise. Some of the answers to those promises take different forms than I expect.

Creator, thank You for the precious gift of expectant anticipation. Help me trust You are fine-tuning that which makes Your presence known. Protect me from impatient static when I don't hear from You immediately. Thank You for countless episodes of Light.

Adjusting my earthly frequency to God's antennae from the lily pad, *Christina*

Christina M. Eder

URGENT WANT, DELAYED RESPONSE

"So the Lord's anger was aroused on that day, and He swore an oath, saying, 'Surely none of the men who came up from Egypt, from twenty years old and above, shall see the land of which I swore to Abraham, Isaac, and Jacob, because they have not wholly followed me' " (Num. 32:10-11).

A bug-eyed stare from the FROG Blog! The Lord got so angry He went back on one of His promises?

I've read about God's wrath, especially in the Old Testament; but after my own recent lag in answering a Godly assignment, Numbers 32:10-11 raised a squirm factor on my lily pad of learning.

My husband and I have frequently been playing Danny Gokey's song, *"Haven't Seen It Yet"* as a reminder of God's faithfulness. We believe He has answers for all our prayer requests, yet we grow impatient while we wait, or a solution doesn't align in a way we expect.

I allow myself to become angry when God delays (according to my constraints), but I'm humbly awakened that I expect Him to patiently accept *my* half-hearted responses. He said He'd be our God if we'd be His people (Jer. 31:33). IF. IF I. IF I. Being God's person means willingly offering Him my whole mind, entire heart, and full spirit commitment. I want quick responses when I call God. Reality check, Christina. God desires quick responses when He calls, too!

In Numbers, God used many methods to guide the Israelites to Canaan. He intended for everyone to enter the Promised Land. God followed through on His leadership plan. But quarreling, distracted, complaining, and insubordinate followers weren't a part of His original plan. His two-way Covenant Street with the Israelites eventually became their one-way Lesson Lane. By not following God's One way, they detoured 40 years through a desert.

God relentlessly pursues us and desires to have our wholehearted honor returned to Him. His passion for us includes delight when we answer Him. His passion involves longing for us to return to Him when we stray. And yes, His passion includes grief and wrath when I rebel or disregard His advances. If I anticipate an unhindered relationship with my Creator as much as He wants it for me, I need to activate this covenant.

God, I thank You for initiating Your faithful promises. Remind me (quickly, please) to reciprocate Your loyalty, especially when I rebel or become distracted. Guard me against choosing a path that is not Your plan. Thank You for your immediate assistance when I recognize I've strayed from Your call.

Yielding on a One-way road that will lead to the eternal Promised Land,

A MARKETING CROSSROAD

"His lord said to him, 'Well done, good and faithful servant; you have been faithful over a few things, I will make you ruler over many things. Enter into the joy of your lord'" (Mt. 25:23).

I defined 2018 as my Year of Intent, and I committed to living 365 days answering my lifelong call to write. Whether I generated income, assignments, or a network, I would be faithful to my purpose. My motto for my Year of Intent became, "I'm so committed to writing I'm willing to live in a tent to live with intent."

In October 2018, my first book, *Life's Too Short for Dull Razors, Cheap Pens, and Worn-Out Underwear*, was finished (after 11 sporadic years of writing, because I wasn't intentional about being an author). I wrote that book for fun, as a double dare from a friend, and for the joy of completing an arduous process. I didn't set out to make a name for myself in the literary arena.

As the book's publishing date drew ever nearer, people asked about social media and marketing. I am an author, not a publicist. I realize some people set out to write for a variety of reasons. My main goal was simply to honor God through writing. To many, this platform sounded naïve, but my focus was strictly to be faithful in finishing the work God began in me as an author.

In looking at Jesus' life, His marketing platform was through the Cross at the top of

Mt. Calvary. He publicized His free love for everyone, yet not everyone signed up for His introductory gift. Jesus spent His first thirty years preparing for publication, three years teaching God's Presence, and He still didn't receive 100% positive feedback. Sometimes, when I read my book reviews, I try to imagine what people of Jesus' time would have posted about His teaching!

Jesus wasn't stymied by the projected numbers of people He'd save or the volume of His words. He remained intent to God's mission and sacrificed positive press – and *everything* else – to show His ultimate public display of affection for us. He gave His all for those who follow Him.

God doesn't ask us to become well-paid servants, well-known servants, well-decorated, or well-reviewed servants. He requests that we become well done, good and faithful servants.

Jesus, thank You for being Author and Editor of my life. I need Your daily revisions so the published work I do through You earns Your best review. Be my Publicist who shares Your writing to people who most need it. Thank You for teaching me the value of loving people more than promotions.

From a fishing net to the internet, I want to faithfully market His gift through my writing on the lily pad,

HELP MY UNBELIEF

"Now He did not do many mighty works there because of their unbelief" (Mt. 13:18).

Matthew 13:18 follows a string of 11 parables Jesus taught about God's priorities. Jesus spoke in parables so only those who chose to receive and apply His spiritually coded message would understand. He spoke in parables, too, so the people, who were a simple folk, would understand the agrarian and servile references. He understood people were at different points in their spiritual walks and would glean different wisdom from each message.

Jesus had – and still has – unlimited resources, but He won't waste them on people who won't utilize His message to lovingly grow the Kingdom of God. The multitudes wanted a message from Jesus but weren't convinced of Jesus' being the One to deliver it. I relate to the multitudes' hesitation because I respond only when I believe in something or Someone. Jesus used parables to discern believers from unbelievers.

Jesus has power plans but will never overpower my free will to follow His works. I want, expect, and wait for His layout design. As I seek to trust God's will, I watch our 8-year-old granddaughter learn to trust Tig and me.

"Gramps, what special plans do you have for us tonight?"

I get to hear Marley Mae ask Tig this question during every dinner. Gramps' time involves teaching through creative play. Grams' time includes errands, house chores, a walk, writing cards to family members, and music while we prepare for dinner. Marley Mae depends on me to pick her up from school and follow a general routine between school and dinner. She anticipates Tig will engage in free play and imaginative activities. Both are crucial for her development.

God uses a similar balance to teach about reliability and spontaneity. He extends an unconditional warranty through His promises. He also allows our life to create changes and surprises. From Marley Mae's perspective, Gramps can do mighty works – like Matthew spoke of about Jesus. She doesn't question *if* Gramps has special plans for their time together. She asks, "*What* special plans do you have for *us*?" She believes Gramps will provide activities they'll experience together. Jesus is loyal to the mighty works He has planned for us if we believe in Him. He doesn't give us His plans and then send us on our way. He goes with us!

Creator, thank You for Your blessed reassurance through the gift of routine. Thank You for crafting surprises into Your plans for my day. Help me believe You are the Perfect Designer, even when I wonder how Your pattern will materialize. Grow my childlike trust to ask, "Abba, what special plans do You have for us today?"

Cleaning algae patches of unbelief out of the lily pad,

Christina

Christina M. Eder

NEED TO WANT

"The Lord did not set His love on you nor choose you because you were more in number than any other people, for you were the least of all peoples; but because the Lord loves you, and because He would keep the oath which He swore to your fathers..." (Dt. 7:7-8).

Relentless. Passionate. Inexhaustible. God chose me *and* set His indelible love on me? Forever? Even after earth passes away?

Tig and I chose one another as lifelong marriage partners nearly 30 years ago. We vowed to love each other "'til death do us part." We chose each other; yet, in our human fragileness, we based our spousal decision on individual needs and wants.

God doesn't have needs, yet He wants me. He chooses me without a guarantee I'll choose to love Him back. Deuteronomy 7:7-8 teaches that God *sets* His love on us and maintains His unconditional promise forever. Marriage calls me to faithfully love my husband; but, unlike God's eternal Vow, our marriage contract expires when one spouse dies.

Tig and I can list many reasons we remain attracted and committed to each other. Sometimes I need to *want* to love him for who he is. God explains He chose me not because I was the most-lovable, richest, most creative (fill in the blank). He claimed me when I was the least. More importantly, He claims me when I am least-lovable, when I'm poor, when

64

I'm uninspired (fill in the blank).

I try to picture people who are dating to deliberately set out to find the least appealing spouse. I can't imagine someone pursuing the least-marketable person to spend their earthly life with, much less live eternally with them. Our relationship decisions point out just how selfishly frail we are, and how generously strong God is. His passion overpowers my vulnerability.

Lord, thank You for choosing me. Please protect me from questioning why You love me when I show up for life less than attractive. Guard me against testing the limits of Your love. Thank You for our relationship that will continue to grow into Eternity.

Setting my loving feet firmly on the lily pad to leap into God's lifelong choices for this FROG,

Christina

CARDIO BOOT CAMP

"Do not let your hearts be troubled. You have faith in God; have faith also in me" (Jn. 14:1 NAB).

In John 14, Jesus is speaking at the Last Supper. I think about Jesus' voice and "hear" Him talking at low volume, moderate pace, and high clarity. He teaches by authority without being domineering.

When I read, "Do not let your hearts be troubled," I try to imagine Jesus as a fitness boot-camp instructor. His warm-up begins with a command to not give in to worry, anxiety, woe, misfortune, suffering, or any form of trouble. Fitness regimes challenge wholehearted stamina. Jesus wants a committed heart, which includes a surrendered one.

"Jesus, I Surrender Myself To You," a prayer written by Fr. Dolinda Ruotolo, teaches "every act of true, blind, complete surrender to Me... resolves all difficult situations." When someone seeks a fitness coach, he is virtually putting his heart on the line. He trusts that coach to strengthen his weakness.

Aerobic exercise involves taking positive steps to help prevent future cardiovascular problems. "Do not let your heart be troubled" is being spiritually proactive. In the same way, a fitness client believes in a coach's expertise, I am instructed to actively trust my Spiritual Coach for matters of the heart.

John 14:1 indicates we are to remain heart healthy. Jesus offered no cool-down period or spiritual muscle breaks when He said, "Do not let..." I think He means forever. Do not (ever, now, or in the future) allow your heart to become distressed.

How can I work out my heart without overtaxing it? Through surrender and trust that God has every move of my earthly workout mapped out. He knows the intensity, weight, timing, and repetitions I can handle to make me a stronger soldier in His boot camp for Him.

Jesus, increase my heart rate to love You and others. Your blood flowed freely for all because You had no clots against anyone. May the oxygen of my soul emit pure air so I can let Your lifeblood flow through me. When I'm tempted to add weight to my heart, remind me to release the tension onto You. Thank You for coaching me to stretch out, flex, run, and endure for Your Eternal Marathon.

As I train for heaven, I'm leaping from the lily pad in a weighted vest of armor,

ELEVATED RESPECT

"Our Father in heaven, Hallowed be Your name" (Mt. 6:9).

I've been doing extensive word studies about surrender. From textbooks, interviews, stories, and personal practice, I've discovered how much courage it takes to submit. I've found surrender is an act of bravery when I apply it in the proper context.

In one word study, I learned hallowed is a form of dependency on someone or something beyond the self. Synonyms for "hallow" include elevate, glorify, raise, consecrate, dignify, upgrade, and honor. In a world where promotions, pay raises, and prestige are alluring, why can it be so difficult to be as captivated by God's Deity?

It takes trust that my house lights will turn on; yet I flip the switch and expect light. It requires surrender to allow for unexpected heating expenses, yet I pay the bill and anticipate future paychecks to recoup the cost. How can I rely on a utility company, but struggle with "Hallowed be Thy name" that Jesus taught in the Lord's Prayer?

I believe part of my hallowing challenge lies in disrespecting lapses between prayer calls and repairs. I treat God like the utility company when I expect Him to get me out of the dark with a flip of a switch. Or when I blow a fuse if He, being Hallowed, answers a prayer differently than I asked.

Perhaps I imagine God will grant all requests as He did in Genesis when He simply said, "Let there be light" and it happened. It's humbling to think that I graciously surrender to a utility company for electricity more than I sometimes trust my Creator to diagnose, fix, and light the entire universe.

Surrender. One word. Countless meanings. Eternal practice. Hallowed be Thy name.

Jesus, thank You for your sovereignty. You have ultimate power and can instantly do everything because You are everything! Mature me to fervently respect Your Deity. Help me accept Your work order response time. Waiting for Thy Kingdom come, practicing His will to be done on an earthly lily pad,

EMOTIONAL TRUTH

"Let him seek peace and pursue it" (1 Pet. 3:11).

"Jesus You take care of everything." I'm participating in a nine-day surrender mission and my daily guide concludes, "Jesus You take care of everything."

Jesus, You take care of everything. Ahhhhhh. Those words saturate my spirit with a peaceful ripple around the lily pad.

I listened to two people separately tell me about recent life speed bumps. One person is weary from an increasing online demand to respond quicker to more people. She said how a once-standard 24-*hour* grace period for non-emergency situations has practically evolved into a 24-*minute* allowance before followup requests ensue. She ended her recap with, "Sometimes I just wish the entire internet would go away." Jesus, You take care of everything.

The other person who shared with me her challenge is highly non-confrontational. This woman is fearless when danger erupts, but for everything else, she encourages broad perspective and logic. In describing her recent chaotic – but non-threatening – encounter, "Michaela" received a deluge of someone else's emotional truth. She defines emotional truth as conversations occurring when low nerves meet high tension. In our talk, she suggested, "The world would be more peaceful if people silently edited their emotional truth and considered the impact before vocalizing them." Jesus, You take care of everything.

In 1 Peter 3:11, he wrote, "Let him seek peace and pursue it." Seek and pursue. Jesus said He left His peace (Jn. 14:27). If I surrender to His peace-filled promise, I know Jesus will take care of everything. It's up to me to trust His serene Truth over my emotional truth.

Jesus, thank You for taking care of everything. When I'm faced with discord, help me conduct myself with the harmony You promise. Help me clearly see Peace where You've left it. Through the Cross, You teach us that "Jesus, You took care of everything."

Seeking calm waters on the lily pad that sits among worldly rip tides,

DETECTING TRASH

"For it is better, if it is the will of God, to suffer for doing good than for doing evil" (1 Pet. 3:17).

During a morning walk, I saw a man scanning a playground with a metal detector (I'm presuming he was looking for something other than a child). With the surplus of empty pizza boxes, soda bottles, and wrinkled decorations, the playground showed evidence of a weekend party.

Even though litter peppered the grounds he was searching, this man's metal detector must not have signaled those already-surfaced treasures. From my vantage point, he willingly dug through potentially buried wreckage but overlooked obvious rubble.

Danish A. Danial said, "Success and failure are both parts of life, but results always depend on your preparation." I don't know what bounty this hunter was tracking, but it didn't appear he regarded litter landmines as trophy bucks. His treasure could have been buried under a pile of unmoved mess.

I may be aware of garbage patrol because when I walk outside, I carry a plastic shopping bag to pick up discarded items. I also get fresh air, exercise, and a cleaner piece of Eden after my strolls. That morning, to avoid interfering with this man's scanning signals, I walked to another section of the park to collect rubbish that needed only a visual detector. (I'm unsure how this man ended his search, but maybe after he finished scanning, he did a clean sweep of the playground).

Trash and treasure. Success and failure. We adopt both sides of a highway when we're born into this world. 1 Pet. 3:17 teaches in doing God's will, it is better to suffer for doing good than for doing evil. I strive to lead with a solution more often than to follow with a problem.

Jesus, thank You for adopting me on Your highway toward eternal life. As I walk among road markers, help me to graciously navigate trials and tribulations. When faced with a choice between trash and treasure, signal me to detect an unpolluted path. Thank You for patiently waiting for me to discover Your riches that are sometimes hidden among worldly rubbish.

Armed with a plastic bag and walking shoes as I jump off the lily pad,

A SHOT IN THE DARK

"In the beginning, when God created the heavens and the earth, the earth was a formless wasteland, and darkness covered the abyss, while a mighty wind swept over the waters" (Gen. 1:1-2).

As an author, I can identify with God's creation story. At the beginning of each writing project, I sometimes see the blank paper as a formless wasteland. The sun may be shining outside while inside I'm waiting for inspiration to fill the abyss between start and finish. I anticipate Holy Spirit wind to sweep over the FROG Blog to stir 500 uplifting words for a lily pad lesson.

I satisfied a friend's double-dare to write a book about what I pondered during distance runs when I wrote my first book, *Life's Too Short for Dull Razors, Cheap Pens, and Worn-Out Underwear.* That literary birthing process took eleven years to reach an undetermined finish line. Every strand of my DNA had been created to write, so the book's deadline became a resurrection to fulfill a mission. I'd allowed years of excuses to waylay God's purpose for me to write publicly.

If God completed projects with the timing and reasoning I sometimes do, the heavens and earth might still be a formless wasteland. Instead, God took His "someday" thoughts and crafted them into "this day's" action.

"This is the day the Lord has made" (Ps. 118:24). God knew He had eternity (and still does) to create, yet He moved when the notion to make heavens and earth stirred Him. If God responded to His Creator role with elapsed time, scripture may read, "There may come a day that the Lord might make. Let's anticipate rejoicing and practice being glad."

Unlike God, my time on earth is limited. When He created in the beginning, He drew me into His plans. I want to use every day to draw nearer to Him. I do that through writing about His creative process at work in my life.

Jesus, thank You for teaching me how to create light openings for dark coverings. Where I am unfocused, shape me into the form You desire. When I allow fear to excuse me from accomplishing Your assignments, nudge me toward completion according to Your timetable. Thank You for writing my life into Your creative plans.

Inviting surrender and trust to sweep me across the waters of the lily pad,

BLINDLY WORKING

"Now as Jesus passed by, He saw a man who was blind from birth. And His disciples asked Him, saying, 'Rabbi, who sinned, this man or his parents, that he was born blind?' Jesus answered, 'Neither this man nor his parents sinned, but that the works of God should be revealed in him' " (Jn. 9:1-3).

My eyes were opened to new perceptions and misconceptions about blindness during Jesus' time on earth. I learned blindness was historically common because of birth defects, leprosy, and infection. Jews associated blindness, and suffering in general, with sin. Some Jews believed in the concept of prenatal sin.

Others surmised parental sins could cause afflictions in a child. (As a teenager, I believed my afflictions originated from Mom and Dad's rules, not from sins I may have committed). Plato introduced an idea that man, in his pre-existent state, may have sinned before conception. (Talk about a future overachiever!)

In Jn. 9:1-3, Jesus never diagnosed the source of this man's blindness. He focused on casting a positive vision for the man's future. The blind man wasn't identified by name, but Jesus knew God would disclose the man's testimony through His Father's eye-opening miracle.

Jesus went to The Cross, fully seeing what He would endure. "No amount of blindness and stumbling can separate us from His love" (Rom. 8:35-39). Original Love. Original sin. Jesus' insight recognizes both. God takes our sin and success to prescribe lenses for life, held together by His unbreakable frame. He will use our vision *and* our blindness to showcase His mighty works.

Jesus, my Original Lens Crafter, thank You for physical vision and strengthening spiritual sight. Open the eyes of my soul to readily see Your wisdom. When I'm blindsided and I slip, guide my weakened night vision to regain clarity. Thank You for Your pure white-tipped Shepherd's crook to lead me into Your fold.

Using depth perception to leap from the lily pad,

DOVE AWARD NOMINATION

"Behold, He struck the rock, so that the waters gushed out, and the streams overflowed. Can He give bread also? Can He provide meat for His people?" (Ps. 78:20).

"Let the groaning of the prisoner come before You; according to the greatness of Your power. Preserve those who are appointed to die; And return to our neighbors sevenfold... so we, Your people and sheep of Your pasture, will give You thanks forever; We will show forth Your praise to all generations" (Ps. 79:11-13).

Poor God. He doesn't need or want our pity. However, I think if anybody deserves a Dove award for best Christian songwriter and producer, it's God.

In Ps. 78:20, I picture Israel rebelling with a somewhat-taunting attitude. The Israelites fully acknowledge God can strike a rock, causing streams to overflow, yet they question whether He can provide bread and meat for them. We judge floods, famine, and worldly conditions according to our limited vantage point. To an unlimited God, His five-star rating isn't affected by audience approval.

Ps. 78:20-72 describes God's fury when the Israelites challenge His credibility. Despite people's disbelief, Psalm 78 shows how God directs everything according to His flawless performance. Immediately following one of God's many "I'll love you no matter what" scenes, Ps. 79:13 stages another doubt-to-belief routine.

For this scripture, I nominate God for a People's Choice Dove award. I vote God as the "Most Followed Producer of the Universe" when His documentary supports my plotline. However, I leave Him off the ballot when I don't think His character is staged according to my scripted cast.

In Ps. 79:13, the people asked God to spare the life of a groaning prisoner on death row. They "graciously" offered God allegiance if He rescued this prisoner. "Return... so we, Your people will give You thanks forever... we will show forth Your praise to all generations." They credit His power and want to be considered His people. However, before they claim a ticket to His eternal showing, they request a trailer from this prisoner-release documentary.

I reflect on how often God sustains me and how quickly I forget His power when I inevitably stumble. I recall patterns of insubordination to my Creative Director when I promised to shape up *after* He showed up. Instead of rehearsing gory monologues from when I act like an Israelite, I close my 500-word scene with audience-participation questions.

How have you practiced trusting God in one situation and reverted to doubt in other situations? When have you promised to follow God's lead after He played His part first?

With encore appreciation measured by God's scale of grace,

JAW BREAKING TRUST

"So the king ordered Daniel to be brought and cast into the lions' den. To Daniel, he said, 'May your God, whom you serve so constantly save you'" (Dan. 6:17).

In an article about releasing control, I learned the more someone attempts to manipulate the outcome, the quicker he becomes agitated when his attempts are thwarted. The article discussed how irritation can throw someone into the jaws of human initiative when they don't allow organic processing. That phrase, "jaws of the human initiative" reminded me of the story of Daniel's being thrown in the lions' den. Different jaws, similar reaction.

I feel like I'm currently wedged in the Jaws of Life as I begin a dual book tour. By simultaneously promoting *Life's Too Short for Dull Razors, Cheap Pens, and Worn-Out Underwear* and an anthology of *The FROG Blog,* I'm readily discovering I'm an author, not (yet) a marketer.

I sell what I believe and use face-to-face interactions or phone calls to endorse people and products. Others have frequently told me individualized strategies are no longer effective or efficient in a technological world. While I learn about posting and podcasting, I feel like my *Martha & Mary Writing Studio* has become Daniel's Lions' Den.

As an amateur marketer, I see modern advertising as jaw-breaking distraction, biting into my writing time. Daniel's story shows me how he lived peacefully among the lions without becoming consumed by them. Daniel was thrown into a pit. I'm wading into an unknown-to-me technological pit. In an author's life, marketing is part of the nature of this beast. Daniel and I both have God in our dens.

Daniel trusted God during his overnight accommodations with the lions and woke to realize he hadn't become their continental breakfast entrée. Meanwhile, I'm waking with restlessness in the pit of my stomach. That gnawing hunger for peace can be filled only with God's protection against my fears of unknown territory. I take a lesson from Daniel, who consistently relied on God – on both sides of the pit.

Jesus, thank You for giving us Daniel's firm example of faith in You. Help me trust Your guardianship to free me from anxious captivity. Protect me from the jaws of this earthly life. Thank You for taming my learning lions while I promote Your written assignments.

From a lily pad, guided by God's market more than by worldly *pit*ches,

Christina

PROTECTED TENSION

"Amos has conspired against you in the midst of the house of Israel. The land is not able to bear all his words" (Amos 7:10).

Conspired. The word conspired often conveys tension. In Denise Sherriff's book, *Kairos Moments,* she comically describes the lesson she learned about setting the sewing machine's tension regulator. Through a difficult (but funny-to-the-reader) lesson, Denise discovered it's crucial to adjust a sewing machine's needle pressure for each project.

In Amos 7:10, the tension between Amos and King Amaziah occurred because authorities of Bethel did not tolerate Amos' prophecy. They accused him of being a traitor, conspiring against their authority. King Amaziah strongly encouraged Amos to return to Judah because the people wouldn't abide by his prophetic words. They thought that if they removed Amos, they'd remove the tension that came with his message. Jesus experienced a similar reception of His word.

Not all pressure derives from unpleasant circumstances (or people). Sherriff explains tension is necessary to hold things together, particularly in family bonds. Within tense environments, the power to love encourages us to loosen our selfishness and tighten our resolve to love another person. She writes, "Tension comes because we don't know how something will be received by others" (Sherriff, Denise. *Kairos Moments.* Derek Press, 2017).

Whether or not Amos knew how his message would be received, I do know he faithfully traveled to Bethel to obey God's assignment. King Amaziah recognized the weight of Amos' message was heavier than the people could handle, but Amos pressed into that tension to further devote himself to his prophetic gift.

I frequently hear, "God won't give you more than you can handle." I haven't been God, so some days I feel I have more than I can handle, but the truth is God won't give me more than He can handle *through* me. After a stressor passes, I often realize my pressure came from a fear that I wouldn't be able to face whatever came my way.

Like the people in Bethel, I cannot handle all of God's words at once. He doesn't ask – nor does He expect – me to control every detail in my land. Like Amos, God faithfully stays in whatever place I'm in when He delivers His message. His mercy isn't threatened when I weakly respond. His grace doesn't conspire against me.

When I allow my free will for God to adjust my tension knob, His peace becomes my protection. He guards me against snapping more than threads when life's fabric is stretched too tight.

Jesus, thank You for being the One whose mission was to bear the weight of the world. You won't give me more than I can handle. Release life's needles of tension threaded by my expectations. Thank You for graciously sewing me into Your pattern of life.

Christina M. Eder

Learning FROG lessons on the lily pad,
one stitch at a time,

Christina

THE FIRST ROCK CONCERT

"And I say to you that you are Peter, and on this rock I will build My church, and the gates of Hades shall not prevail against it" (Mt. 16:18).

Jesus may have been the Original Rock Promoter. He called Peter a rock to build His church upon. Can you imagine Jesus saying He believed in you enough to invite you to lead His worldwide tour? It'd be the ultimate Rock of Ages offer! Jesus also presented Peter a sign-on bonus with an unconditional guarantee that whatever hell His 12 band members faced, Hades would not prevail.

Peter jumped onto Jesus' tour bus in Matthew 16:18. Together, their motley crew developed a following as they invited people to experience a Real Light show. Jesus booked additional tour dates and offered Truth and Wisdom tickets to be eternally redeemed.

Jesus knew He'd close out His farewell tour on Good Friday. Before He retired, Jesus celebrated His band's three-year history with a Bread and Wine party. After their Last Supper together, Jesus walked with His disciples to the Garden of Gethsemane. He knew His departure process would be immensely painful, so He chose Peter and two friends to pray with Him.

Jesus explained Peter would deny Him three times before He retired; Peter adamantly said he'd rather die than deny Jesus (Mt. 26:33-35). However, Jesus knew Peter would so long I wander from my One True Love.

The Israelites worshipped wood and stone. Gomer idolized men to whom she was not married. I'm enamored by neatly packaged plans and dreams. Wood, stone, Hosea, agendas, and self-seeking aspirations are incapable of the unconditional love only God can deliver.

I'm humbled to think if I followed God with the intensity with which He pursues me, I wouldn't be as enticed to chase distractions that haven't bled for me. As a child of the King, blood is thicker than water. I want His Lifeblood to flow through me, and to live eternally for His Kingdom.

Jesus, thank You for faithfully leading me, even when I follow unfaithful things. As a bride of Christ, purify my mind, soul, and body. Train me to be a faithful wife to You. Thank you for Hosea's example of relentless love.

Worshipping the Rock and Cornerstone of my lily pad,

STEPPIN' UP TO FLY HIGHER

"The steps of a good man are ordered by the Lord, and He delights in his way" (Ps. 37:23).

A shrieking bird made me dash to the window to look for the source of this feathered frenzy's distress. The bird continued crying so I stepped closer, hoping my presence would scare the predator away or encourage the bird to move toward safety. Either way, I wanted to relieve this bird's 911 tweet.

I tested Newton's third law of motion: Every action produces an opposite or equal reaction. The theory withstood the test as I saw how my strides caused that bird and numerous others to flee. Rabbits, squirrels, and a dog walker's now-agitated canine, had all been affected by one bird's motion. I wondered how that scenario would have played out had I remained a passive bystander by the window?

How have others' outcome been changed with a few words, a small action, or a silent expression? Psalms 37:23 says the steps of a good man are ordered by the Lord. (This scripture doesn't specify what happens to the steps of a bad man).

Did my ordered steps that particular day include those dozen paces that changed animal behavior? The predator may have been upset that my order probably caused him to miss a meal. The bird may have been relieved because my motion elevated him to safety. The bird had the ability to leave the situation at be out of tempo with His sold-out show that night. He also knew Peter would eventually rebound from buckling under his stage fright.

After their prayer, Jesus went solo. And Peter went to sleep. Jesus returned from praying to find His sleeping beauties oblivious to His pending betrayal. Judas had temporarily left the band after Supper and now returned to give Jesus an arresting kiss on His cheek.

I wonder if Peter's silent watch during Jesus' arrest foreshadowed his rejection. From a comfortable judgment seat, it's easy to question how Peter's rock-solid loyalty had quaked. Jesus wasn't surprised. If I had been in Peter's spotlight and my faith show was displayed, I'd be relieved only three of my discrepancies were featured.

Jesus continued trusting Peter's devotion until death. After His Resurrection, He offered Peter a rain-date ticket for a comeback performance. During that redemption event, Jesus asked Peter three times if he loved Him. Peter, although he may have felt (black) sheepish, affirmed his love. Jesus overrode Peter's three denials with three invitations to show love. They both received a standing ovation that brought Heaven down.

Jesus, thank You for using Peter's denial to teach me about Your redemption. When I become self-assured about my undying love for You, remind me everyone can crumble under crowd pressure. I eagerly look forward to Your reunion tour!

Leaping around Rocks and Living Water,

MY BAAL

"On that day, says the Lord, She shall call me 'My husband,' and never again 'My baal' " (Hos. 2:18).

Baal has never surfaced as one of my conversational titles. Occasionally when my husband says he needs to talk to me, I jokingly respond, "Speak, lord, your servant is listening." He's temporarily humored when I refer to him as "lord." And note it's lowercase *lord.* We also laugh because he knows I'm not falsely idolizing him.

I learned "baal" means master, and was an honorary term wives historically used to acknowledge their husbands as lord over their house. The prophet Hosea spoke to the Israelites who worshipped false gods, including the pagan god Baal. They had associated Lord and Baal for so long, they saw little or no difference between the real God and their lowercase god.

Hosea's story describes his unfortunate marriage to Gomer, an adulteress. Though she was habitually unfaithful, Hosea's duty to faithfully love his wife drove him to find her. He took Gomer back, but with conditions.

Like the Israelites, I've sadly served some false gods long enough that I've allowed my worship of Baal and Lord to sit close on the same altar. Like Gomer's character, I fall into the arms of my agenda. I chase the success of a completed checklist. I date other priorities because they appear to be weighted with muscle. I've maintained these affairs for any time. I didn't do anything to help it flee. It was merely my steps that set the flight into motion.

My walk is prepared by my Creator. He includes free will in His marching instructions. I've found my fight-or-flight impulse soars when I'm tuned in to listen, move, or wait for His Presence.

Holy Spirit, thank You for mapping out my life's course. May I desire to align with Your flight pattern. Make me aware of seen or unseen vultures that threaten peaceful doves. Thank You for people who have stepped into my path to help me fly, especially when I've been threatened by inner scavengers.

Making a motion to adjourn from today's lily pad,

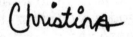

ASYLUM

"Select for yourselves cities to serve as cities of asylum" (Num. 35:11).

In Moses' day, cities of asylum were established across the Jordan and into the land of Canaan. Numbers 35:9-32 maps out criteria to decipher between intentional or accidental death. These refuge cities served as protection for people who unintentionally killed someone.

A city of asylum. A place where the innocent can be free from headhunters. I'd love to have a safe place to rest my head, primarily from battering thoughts.

Living in a world that is plugged in and tuned out sometimes feels like an assault against kindness. There's abundant motion but not necessarily gentle emotion. And this culture of mercy killing leaves war marks. We need compassionate healing.

God established a global day of asylum known as the Sabbath Day. He instructs us to honor this weekly vacation day to step out of a murderously paced world. We are called to unplug and tune in to God's peaceful energy. Jesus gave us a gift of respite when He said in John 14:27, "peace I leave with you, My peace I give to you." (Nowhere in scripture does it indicate He came back to reclaim that promise, so I must remember to pick up that peace.)

Christian believers are treated to asylum because God's grace covers us. Grace shelters forgiveness even when we intentionally or accidentally murder in action, words, or lack of

91

action. Mercy is another sanctuary God built into His peace talks. We dwell in Mercy City because we can count on His love, despite our innumerable sins.

Jesus, thank You for safe havens like Your peace, mercy, and grace. I confess I don't deserve these gifts, yet You invite me to wrap myself in Your protective packaging. Help me regularly appreciate Your safety zones. Thank You for Your compassion as I travel toward a Permanent Residency of eternal rest.

Protected like an endangered species and joyfully leaping from the lily pad,

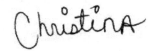

UNCLE!

"They received from Moses all the contributions which the Israelites had brought for establishing the service of the sanctuary. Still morning after morning the people continued to bring their voluntary offerings to Moses. Thereupon the experts... told Moses, 'The people are bringing much more than is needed to carry out the work which the Lord has commanded us to do.'

"Moses, therefore, ordered a proclamation... 'Let neither man nor woman make any more contributions... So the people stopped bringing their offerings; there was already enough at hand, in fact, more than enough, to complete the work to be done" (Ex. 36:3-7).

Too many contributions? More than enough helpers? These are problems building campaigns long for! Ample resources seem foreign in a country where "Now Hiring" signs replace "Welcome" mats on many storefronts. Moses told the people all worker positions had been filled. He asked the community to stop bringing supplies because they were overstocked.

Moses cried uncle when he proclaimed the sanctuary project had overabundant provision. I have yet to experience a telethon that concludes its fundraising efforts ahead of schedule. I have never seen a donation refund issued, due to overpayment. The Israelites voluntarily gave their time, sweat equity, and resources to engrave unity in stone.

The Lord appointed Moses to build this sanctuary. Moses' obedience led others to commit to his ordained mission. They not only pledged contributions but fully endorsed their promise. I have been part of capital campaigns in which commitment cards diminish to suggestion appeals. Initially, red-hot donors have turned lukewarm, or colder, when project deadlines come due. Perhaps it was because they were not truly sold on the purpose of our efforts. Exodus 36:3-7 shows what can happen when people plan and work together toward a Greater Purpose.

Jesus, thank You for providing modern-day leaders who, like Moses, build upon Your assignments. Strengthen my resolve to follow through when I'm presented with a serving opportunity. Help me contribute to Your Kingdom crusades from the loving heart You unselfishly give to me. Thank You for Your foundational allegiance in Word and action.

Bringing pledges and offerings to life's lily pad,

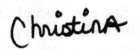

SHOPPING FOR SOUL FOOD

"For this command which I enjoin on you today is not too mysterious and remote for you. It is not up in the sky, that you should say, 'Who will go up in the sky to get it for us and tell us of it, that we may carry it out?'... No, it is something very near to you, already... in your hearts; you have only to carry it out" (Dt. 30:11-14).

My pie-in-the-sky love note would read: "Grocery shopping is finished. I picked up all the items from your list and put everything away. The table is set. See you after work."

I like to plan meals. I love cooking and baking. I'm less enthused about budgeting, shopping, loading, unloading, and putting away groceries as part of my kitchen desire. I humor myself into thinking shopping is simply the salty part of a recipe to flavor what makes meal preparation delicious to me.

The soul ingredients from Deuteronomy 30:11-14 blend into stick-to-my-ribs food for my mind. By using His original recipe to serve His will from the table of Life, God marinates my heart and mouth with crafted seasonings. Out of love for us, He completed the proverbial grocery-shopping process so I get to prepare satisfying meals to serve others.

God clearly reveals His will in my heart so I can easily remember it. He feeds my mouth with His provisions for love so I can readily talk about it. No special interpreter is required to bring the will of God to people. A delegated messenger is not necessary to speak God's message. An obedient heart and ears are basic ingredients to bake love into a hungry world.

Jesus, thank You for inviting me into Your fully furnished kitchen of compassion and kindness. Help me to serve up generous portions of gentleness and care every day. Guard me against dishing out stingy rations of patience and peace. Thank You for Your commitment to keep my house fully supplied so I may feed others.

Serving from a buffet of God's grace, mercy, and love on the lily pad,

NO AMOUNT OF HORSEPOWER
WILL BREAK MY STRIDE

"God takes no delight in the strength of horses, no pleasure in the runner's stride" (Ps. 147:10 NAB).

"He does not delight in the strength of the horse; He takes no pleasure in legs of a man" (Ps. 147:10).

Say it isn't so! One verse, two messages; two versions, one meaning. Psalm 147:10 embodied Tig's and my individual passions: vehicles and racing for him; running and hiking for me. This scripture refers to the horses God created; the 300-450 horses Tig rides are man-powered and saddled beneath the hoods of vehicles. For me, a day without leg power for outdoor exercise grinds my creative energy to a halt.

God created horses. God created legs. However, I don't think God is impressed with horses or legs beyond the purpose for which He designed them. Life often bucks me off a saddle when I use my individual strength as the driving force. Parents, the media, a spouse, pastor, teacher, or friend can offer limited short-term strength, but it's only God's power that eternally sustains us.

I used two translations of Psalms 147:10 to make sure God meant what He said about not taking pleasure in runner strides. So much for my Fully Relying On God when I check His message's consistency just because

I'm uncomfortable with the message it's teaching.

After countless miles and hours of training to run with endurance, one of the last things I want to read is that God takes no pleasure in a gazelle stride or personal
records. If my spiritual core is weak, the entire body is only artificially strong.

Like horsepower, relying on leg strength looks different to each person. By trusting job, money, success, education, or other external platforms to bear our weight, we risk missing God's muscle. By defining machine power to rate performance, we drive dangerously against God's Engine Capacity.

Horses are important. Legs are also important. God is most important. When I maintain this posture of priority, I can be continually strengthened to run or ride with His horse-powered magnitude.

Jesus, thank You for your perpetual strength. There's nothing I can do that will give You more pleasure than completely releasing my heart to You. Be my spiritual fitness coach and strength train me from the inside out.

Hitting my stride and taking pleasure and delight in God's power to reinforce the foundation of my lily pad,

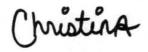

SILENCE ISN'T ALWAYS GOLDEN

"As long as I kept silent, my bones wasted away; I groaned all the day. For day and night your hand was heavy upon me; my strength withered as in dry summer's heat. Then I declared my sin to you; my guilt I did not hide. I said, 'I confess my faults to the Lord, and you took away the guilt of my sin' " (Ps. 32:3-5).

Admission. Emergency call. Confession. Cry.

Each of these words can draw a different picture, based on individual experiences. The bottom line indicates recognizing the need to surrender to another person's help. It can be challenging to admit our weakness or to ask forgiveness in times of struggle. Reasons for limitations vary: lack of education, lack of health, lack of discretion, lack of wise choices.

In a hospital, patients are admitted until they are healed or capable of recovery at home. In broad terms, patients recognize they are incapable of caring for themselves at that time. Medical staff and emergency workers are trained to aid when they are notified or see a situation where they can assist. Unless a person reaches out, often he will remain in pain. We are called to action, even in our weakness.

The same relationship applies to God and His believers. Unless we admit we caused damage or received harm, we remain afflicted. The writer of Psalms 32 talked about his bones wasting away, strength waning, and vitality withering because of his heavy heart. He'd not yet made a confessional 911 call, and until he admitted himself into God's hospital, he was weighted with sin-related guilt.

In an emergency dispatch center, the operator will ask the caller to remain on the phone line until help arrives. Sometimes God waits to engage a rescue mission until we initiate a cry for Him. He stays on the line, protecting us with His reassuring presence, reminding us assistance is coming but the waiting time may sometimes be longer than expected.

Often, my unwillingness and rebellion delay my ultimate pain relief. Just because I don't acknowledge my wrongdoing or wrong speaking doesn't conceal my sin. Ignoring the infection of guilt only makes a heart condition worse.

God's infinite faithfulness is able to meet every need without judging whether the nature of sin or the intensity of trauma is worth forgiving. Jesus is my referral for any sin condition, and I'm covered under His perfect health plan. As soon as I notice symptoms of weakness, loss of joy, restlessness, fatigue, or heaviness in my bones, I am to immediately consult my Physician. His rescue operators are standing by to take my call.

Remembering to keep God as my #1 in the lily pad's speed-dial contacts,

Christina

THE UNDERSIDE OF THE LILY PAD

"I'm not much of a writer."

"I'm not good at putting words together."

"I can't write as well as he/she does."

"Ya know, I've been meaning to write down some things to pass along to my kids, but I don't know what to include."

"That's a loaded question. I have no clue where to start writing a story!"

"I have a lot going on right now and I'm not sure I can commit to this project."

"Yes, but I'll need a ton of help."

"Funny you called, because I've been reflecting on my life in broader terms lately."

These were some responses I received when I invited these authors to join me on the second book in this FROG Blog series. I relate to and understand their initial hesitation, because I had more than 35 years of professional experience delaying my calling to write professionally. That's more than 12,775 days to sell myself on "reasons" why I wasn't qualified to write. All those excuses and rationalization fed only one predator invading life's lily pad: FEAR. I had to fire every one of those lies to fearfully – albeit purposefully – jump into fresh waters.

These fears still knock on my door, but now, instead of rolling out the welcome mat, greeting them with a smile and a plate of warm cookies, I say, "No soliciting!" I write these "reasons" for my delay of the writing game to expose light on dark thoughts.

Fear of comparison (comparing myself

and being compared to past, present, and even future authors)

Fear of failure (surprisingly, that's more understandable than fear of success because, in my mind, I'm more experienced in handling failure than success)

Fear of success (What if I live my writing dream only to find it's just a hidden nightmare?)

Fear of judgment (What will Dad say? Will biblical scholars scoff at my approach to teaching about relying on God? What if I write about what I've learned and then have a setback to living that lesson? Will I be labeled a hypocrite?)

Fear of cost (publishing costs, editors, illustrators, ISBNs, marketing. I live frugally, but realistically, I only have so many recipes for ramen noodles and microwave popcorn to sustain me.)

Fear of prioritizing (What's necessary? What's fluff? Do I write for myself? Do I write for others? When do I write? In what order do I tackle projects?)

Fear of technology (Tech NO LOGIC gaps are slowly being filled through a sharp learning curve, but it's still a weakness)

Fear of social media (as an introvert, "social" *anything* becomes my mass-media release!)

I keep that list to reference past fears and how I continue to face and overcome them. As I've progressed in my writing career, I've discovered none of these fears is new. The concerns I face are the same, but each fear is simply hiding behind a different mask.

Fast forward past my journey, because it's time to introduce these courageous FROG authors. Twelve initially hesitant people joined me, with 13 of us singing a variation of the "Where do I start?" chorus.

After months of tedious tenacity – and God's spirit – we've re-formed our trepidation as transformation. These stories are just the beginning. We finish only when we start.

The following stories represent individual artists sharing their Fully Rely On God stories. To maintain authenticity of the artists' craft, I have asked my editors and publisher to limit corrections to spelling and print formatting. I am humbled by their willingness to say yes, even when their reasoning said no. We all encourage each other to walk strong daily, using earth's journey to practice for heaven.

Using our daily walk as training grounds to practice FROG living on life's (Frozen) Lily Pad,

Christina

NOT A SHADOW OF A DOUBT
Mary Ballinger

I've often thought about a God's-eye
view of the people He created with finite detail.

He sees connections from one generation
to the next. The microscopic chromosomes,
the DNA of each.

He made each individual with talents
and tendencies and placed each human in
their own special time and place.

We are all different with each moment of
experiences molding our being.

God sees us as we are, His omniscient
gaze examines.

Does He love some more than others?
Did He create favorites?

No, I believe He loves us equally, perhaps
seeing us as shadows down on earth.

From God's view we have no different
color skin, nor faces beautiful or dull.

But surely God sees us covered in a
shade of sinfulness.

And beauty is only brought to surface
as we let his Son inside us.

And shadows disappear with His radiant
light of grace.

With grace comes perspective that we
need this loving Father to forgive us and erase
the dark to let our souls blossom.

I've not a shadow of a doubt that God is
my Creator and that He shared his Son with
me to bring color to this world.

DON'T BE A TOAD – TRUST AND TAKE THE LEAP
Tom Ballinger

As a young father, my life focus was to be a provider for our family:
Food, Clothes, Shelter, Education
Love—Love—Love
Security, Comfort
Support, Encouragement
Fun, Happiness, Laughter
Solid Foundation of Christian Faith
Lead and Teach by Example
Discipline, Obedience
Trust, Forgiveness

The blessed, rich life of raising children and experiencing the joy that is our family is not my story though. My story is about what I came to learn from the consummate spiritual role model of Christ-like love though my wife and the family whom God blessed me with. My story is about the journey of learning to fully trust in God.

I put together the outline above as I pondered what I've learned based around my life experiences. In the past, my initial response would have been a puffed-out chest full of pride when asked, "How'd it go?" or "How'd they turn out?" Reflecting from further down the road of my faith journey, gratitude and "Praise be to God" rise above pride to the top of the human-emotion pool.

"Every good and perfect gift is from above, coming down from the father of the heavenly lights, who does not change like the shifting shadows" (Jm. 1:17).

I believe this comes slower for us men, for whom God seemingly used extra-heavy gauge wire during our design phase. Thus, that pride thing still bubbles up in the pond far too often. Men as problem solvers, doers and fixers vs. listeners, ponderers and nurturers may be a stereotype, but for me, it has merit. I believe it adds to the challenge of letting go and truly placing full trust in God. Reflecting on my life experiences, I realize how God was using this family (that I believed was my responsibility to shape and mold) to shape and mold me, pointing me toward a more personal relationship with Him, one I believe He designed for us and desires with each of us.

"God, I have no idea where I am going. I do not see the road ahead of me. I cannot know for certain where it will end. Nor do I really know myself... But I believe that the desire to please you does in fact please. And I hope I have that desire in all that I am doing. Therefore, I will trust you always though I may seem to be lost... I will not fear, for you are ever with me, and you will never leave me to face my perils alone." – Thomas Merton

I have come to realize virtually everything I do now, as part of my faith journey, was modeled or inspired by my wife or one of my children earlier in my life. Our Big Daddy is truly in control of His perfect plan, and His will indeed be done!

So, the example from this cheesy segue is that Christian music plays a prominent role in my life today. It's what I listen to 90 percent of the time. We've gone to many concerts and music festivals. This seed was planted nearly 20 years ago when one of my daughters gave me a Big Daddy Weave CD. She purchased it at Life Fest, thinking I might like it and because the chubby, bearded lead singer (Mike Weaver) reminded her of me. Today, they are my favorite band and I find their songs to be scripturally inspired and many are deeply moving for me. Who knew? Our Big Daddy did, that's who!

While growing up, and as a young husband and father, reading the bible just wasn't something I did very often. Fortunately, God had a beautiful plan to fix this. He filled my daughters and eventually my wife with a passion to read and study scripture. Praise God! Daily scripture and ongoing bible study are now mainstays of my faith life. The bible lifts my eyes to God and teaches me to take a long-term view. I grow in the power of Christ as I study His Word, follow his example and draw closer to him through prayer.

The following are a few meditations and prayers I use to prepare myself to hear what God has to tell me and teach me.

Scripture teaches twin truths:

1. God chose us in Him [Christ] before the creation of the world (Eph. 1:4).

2. Yet we are responsible to believe. Both the divine and the human are at work in everyone who comes to Jesus.

Faith is a gift, but God does not do the believing for us. Truth that exceeds the grip of our minds is within the grasp of our faith.

"Lord, thank you for your Word. It is filled with the truth about your marvelous and amazing ability and desire to save us. Help me not only to see deeper into your Word, but also to be a doer of what you reveal. May none of your Truths be lost to casual eyes. I ask you for Your strength and patience to look intently at your sayings.

In Jesus' name I pray—Amen"

(Steven Chapman, *A Look at Life from a Deer Stand*)

One of the most joyful and rewarding developments of letting go and learning to trust God has come from an opportunity to become more involved with some amazing mission and charity projects. Upon further review, the foundation for these missions was again being poured right before my eyes in years gone by. As I mentioned earlier, I have been blessed with a wife who is my live-in compassionate who can't say no to anyone in need. She is a spiritual role model of Christ-like love. Through the years, our kids have all been involved in a wide variety of endeavors, ranging from special-needs camp counseling to various foreign and domestic mission work.

"I was blind but now I see." This famous song lyric rings so true the more I remember to trust and leave things in God's hands. Easy to say, but hard to do for a human sinner like me. My favorite quote comes from Fr. Bill Matzek, an amazing spiritual mentor and role model (now working from the home office on high). He said, "If you want to make God laugh, tell him *your* plans." Another favorite quote hangs in our kitchen: "Leave everything in God's hands and eventually you'll see God's hand in everything."

Five years ago, a work colleague from back in the late '80s contacted me, out of the blue, and asked whether I might be interested in helping him out with a charitable project called Mission Mobility. A couple years earlier, Rick had gone on a mission trip to Guatemala and was subsequently told by the director of that ministry, "God told me you were going to find wheelchairs for us in the United States!"

Rick's initial response was, "I'm a farmer in Iowa. I don't know a thing about wheelchairs!"

Fast forward. To date, Mission Mobility has sent 32 pods full of wheelchairs, food and clothing to Guatemala. This past January I was blessed to participate in my fourth trip to Guatemala and am still helping gather chairs and supplies wherever I can. As Rick often says, "Praise God, all I did was say yes. He takes care of the rest."

The stories are numerous and powerful of how God has worked to change lives through Mission Mobility, Bethel Ministries, and On His Path. They are a testimony to what God can do when we say yes and then step out of the way and trust in Him. I first thought that was where I'd go with this project, but somehow (I think we know how), I found myself reflecting on how God brought me to this point in my journey via my life experiences. Another fruit of God's handiwork in reuniting Rick and me is how close our relationship as brothers in Christ has grown in five years.

How does that happen? Same answer. Take the leap, say yes to God, and completely trust Him.

"The world's way of pursuing riches is grasping and hoarding. You attain My riches by letting go and giving. The more you give yourself to Me and My ways, the more I fill you with inexpressible, heavenly Joy."

(Sarah Young, *Jesus Calling*)

When we trust in Him, He will use us and the gifts and talents he's provided to share the gospel through our life experiences in ways and with people we don't even realize. We just have to trust that it so, because he says it is!

"*I am made* in God's image, with an ability to respond and relate to God.

I am filled with the Holy Spirit. And God is at work in me through the problems and pressures I face today.

I am part of God's plan. Therefore, what I do today has significance eternally."

(Ray Steadman, *From Guilt to Glory*)

LIFE IS A PILGRIMAGE
Brenda Brandt

We all came from God and, hopefully, our main goal is to return to Him. Although on some level I might have known this earlier, it was later when I took it more seriously.

Life is a pilgrimage and it becomes evident that we encounter hills, valleys, and possibly deserts. While the hills and valleys are difficult to navigate, the mountaintop experiences give me joy, encouragement and hope. While visualizing how my journey might look to God, I am confronted with a messy image. Fortunately, God has a better vantage point and knows His plans for me.

I am not confident I've ever "fully relied on God." One of my first tests was when my husband, Dennis, and I were longing for a family. After fertility testing, my doctor said, "I can't tell you that you will never have children, but if you were, you probably would have by now. Have you considered adoption?"

Until this point, life was going well, giving me the sense I had control. But during a three-week trip in Mexico I told God I was willing to give up traveling if only we could have a child. During subsequent fertility tests and the adoption process, Dennis and I realized we were not fully in control. Our faith life stepped up a few notches! Countless prayers were frequently invoked.

In May 1980, while driving less than a mile from home, I turned a sharp corner, heading down a hill, when a logging truck, partially on my side of the road, barreled toward me. In a terrifying second, I felt this would be the end of my life. I shouted, "Oh God!" When my car stopped, I realized I was alive and could see the sky above me. The hook at the back of the truck caught my car above the rearview mirror and peeled the roof back. It was miraculous that, although the car was totaled, I didn't have any injuries. There was no doubt God had spared my life. I wondered why.

That answer came two months later, when the social worker from the adoption agency called to ask if we were ready to bring our baby girl home. The next day, at the adoption agency, they placed a precious two-month old girl with a pink-yarn hair bow in my arms. It was love at first sight!

Although Dennis and I trusted God to answer our family's prayers, He did so beyond our expectations! And four years later, it was Dennis who fielded the call from the adoption agency. He surprised me by presenting a note that congratulated me on becoming the mom of a second daughter!

Eight years after our first adoption, God really surprised us (and everyone else!) when I learned I was pregnant. Little did we know that after beginning parenthood through adopting, I would deliver a healthy baby girl at the age of 40! Both adopting and delivering a child were equally rewarding experiences and a blessing!

After 36 years of ups and downs of a somewhat-normal married life, we faced our biggest challenge. In January 2010, I noticed

Dennis sometimes needed to cough to finish a sentence. Five months later, he agreed to see a doctor. In November, testing began as more symptoms appeared. He was treated locally, but now we were visiting various VA locations. In January, 2011 we learned he had cancer. In February he was informed of stage-4 lung cancer caused by a genetic defect. It had spread to his liver, brain and bones.

After the diagnosis, we sought palliative care. The first doctors recommended Dennis go through whole-brain radiation before chemotherapy. He declined their recommendations, after having watched his sister face countless treatments one year prior. He explained his decision to our daughters and extended family: "I have lived a good life and have done about all I wanted to do. If this is God's will, I'm ready to go." Although I understood his point of view, it was very hard for us to hear his decision.

During the months Dennis was in hospice, his sister, a nurse, was in research frenzy to find a chemo pill to treat his cancer. Her efforts resulted in learning the FDA had just approved Xalkori, a recently developed drug.

We met the doctor who told Dennis, "You have not been the traditional patient. I didn't expect to see you here in September!"

After explaining this new drug, Dennis said, "Sign me up!"

One of our daughters was with us and we looked at each other in amazement, since he hadn't made a quick decision in months.

The three of us left the appointment with hope that we hadn't experienced for so long.

Two days later, that hope became elevated when I called in to the *Drew Mariani Show* on Relevant Radio. I asked for prayers that our insurance company would pay for the costly drug to treat Dennis. Five minutes after we finished the chaplet, I received the amazing news that they would! There could be no doubt that once again, prayers were being answered!

A few days later, the doctor gave us a prescription for Xalkori, but since the drug was so new, it was only managed by a pharmacy in Indiana. Meanwhile, Dennis' left lung had collapsed and filled with fluid.

Soon after the Xalkori arrived, we noticed improvements with Dennis' increased weight and energy level. We knew even though Xalkori could improve his quality of life, it was not a cure! The following 15 months were a continual roller-coaster ride, but the extra time allowed him to give one daughter away in marriage, and take a vacation in Maine.

On December 1, 2012, my dear Dennis completed his pilgrimage on earth and is now reaping his eternal rewards. One of the first and best pieces of advice I received soon after his diagnosis was to keep a list of blessings, large and small. Because of that, I found myself being more observant of the ways God was providing for our family.

I'll always treasure some of the words Dennis left us. He had written, "Perhaps the Lord permits me to suffer temporarily in order to add a stronger dimension of spirituality to family, friends and others I meet." That observation became more profound than he realized. But my favorite remains something he said after receiving the Sacrament of Anointing and Apostolic Blessing: "I'm so lucky to have friends, family and relatives accompanying me on this journey of life. I'll try to help you on your journey to heaven." Since that day, there have been times when I've felt his assistance, especially in his example of fully relying on God.

Taking a pilgrimage had never been on my bucket list. However, as more of my friends ventured to and returned from the Holy Land, I felt an increased pull. I was concerned about my safety, but my friends reassured me about their experiences and I realized I needed to trust God to protect me. I was scheduled to leave for the Holy Land in March 2015, but the day before my flight, my mother called to say my 96-year-old dad had been taken to the hospital. I drove down to see my dad, and as soon as I arrived, I knew his time on earth was short. I cancelled my trip.
My mother, siblings and I were there when he peacefully completed his pilgrimage.

Although I never regretted that decision, I was faced with hesitancy as to whether God really wanted me to go to the Holy Land, and whether it was safe enough to go. It took over a year to resolve those two questions and sign up again. By the time I decided to go, the group was filled. The leader asked if I wanted to go on a waiting list. I couldn't decide, so I declined. Eventually, I called back and was able to purchase a ticket. In 2016, I celebrated Christmas and my birthday in Bethlehem!

God has a way of outdoing Himself and surpassing our expectations. As a result of that pilgrimage and programs in our parish, my desire to return to the Holy Land increased. I said to God, "If you don't want me to return, please take this desire from me!" Fortunately, He didn't and two years later, one of my daughters joined me for a pilgrimage that surpassed the first! This time we celebrated Mass in the Tomb of Christ on my birthday. Only God, and my dear husband, could have planned those two special birthdays!

With hills, mountains, valleys, and deserts still ahead of us, the pilgrimage of life continues because God isn't finished yet! I am in full agreement with one of Dennis' final comments, "I'm so lucky to have friends, family and relatives accompanying me on this journey of life. I'll try to help you on your journey to heaven."

VALLEYS AND MOUNTAINS
Todd Eder

As I sit atop an outlook to the Grand Canyon, I reflect on its beauty, but nothing compares to the awe of being a father to my three daughters. I think about what I'd like to pass on to them about life and am reminded of a saying my granny instilled in my heart before she passed in 2015. "You gotta believe." Those three words might seem cliché to some people, but to me, they mean everything.

My oldest daughter, Marley, turned eight in February. Despite life's challenges of anger, fear, and anxiety, the most important thing I've passed on to her is to always keep love in your heart. I work on the road for a living, which is very difficult, but we always remind each other to keep that love in our hearts and "you gotta believe."

My middle daughter, Teagan, is seven years old and growing up quickly as she progresses through life. I'm excited to help her through her adventures and to keep believing.

My youngest daughter, Ellie, is two, but when she gets old enough to understand this lesson, I can't wait to pass it down to her and continue to watch all my beautiful girls grow.

You gotta believe!

UNDER MARY'S MANTLE
Elizabeth Demos Garibaldi

I release my past and all its pain to God's Mercy: dreams, desires, sufferings, sins and sorrows, yes and even joys and delights. I lay them down at the foot of the Cross and allow Christ's Precious Blood to flow over me like a river, washing me clean... breaking the chains, healing my wounds... opening my eyes, my ears, my heart, my very soul, to receive His Mercy.

Embraced by Love, I ignite my desire to be His, embracing unshakeable confidence in my identity and purpose as His beloved daughter.

I sit in silence in the church at the Shrine of Our Lady of Guadalupe, in La Crosse, Wisconsin. Before me is Magnificence: A mosaic of the Blessed Mother, towering over the Real Presence of Jesus in the golden Tabernacle. A crucifix and angels loom thirty feet above. They cast their loving gazes upon me. Such love and compassion bring peace and a smile to me.

Few linger after Mass. They stay at the foot of the Cross to utter words only the heart can hear.

I sit consoling Jesus' pierced, burning Sacred Heart... and Mary's pierced, sorrowful Immaculate Heart. I feel love and deep gratitude from them and for them.

Suddenly, sunlight penetrates the dim light in the church, cast by a sky of thick clouds.

The beams of light cascading through the windows in the high dome above envelop me. I close my eyes, letting the beams' warmth penetrate. Too bright, the brilliant light sears straight to my soul and warms my heart.

Bathed in celestial love, I am transported beyond the burdens of sorrows, sins and grief with which I have so many times journeyed to this sanctuary.

The dark clouds part; the sun warms my eyelids again. I am back in the pew, alone with my Lord and my Blessed Mother; I feel Mary's presence. She knows and has felt the pain of every sorrow. She reaches out to me through the sunbeam and wipes away the tears that stream silently down my cheeks, wrapping me in her comforting, protective mantle.

The words embroidered on my pillowcase saturated with sleep and tears, come to mind: "Listen and be sure... That I will protect you, do not be frightened, or let your heart be dismayed... Am I not here? I, who am your mother. And is not my help a refuge?"

A cloud obscures the sun again. I open my eyes to absorb in awe the artistry and angels around me: The Magnificent Mosaic of Mary, My Mother... the pillars and paintings, statues, saints and silence – all inspired by the ultimate act of Love, Mercy and Perfect Obedience to God's Will.

HALF THE MAN
Brian Jeffords

When I growing up in the small village of Holmen, Wisconsin, I was blessed to have many wonderful influences in my life. I would love to be half the people they were and are.

The first one is my father, Frank. He is a wonderful example of what it is to be a Christian, day in and day out. He is always so welcoming of everyone he meets and a vivid example of what Jesus wants us to be and how to treat those around us. He helped plan and lead our church youth group on a mission trip to Milwaukee to work with Habitat for Humanity and former president Jimmy Carter. On that trip, I watched him sharing all the knowledge he learned growing up with the local families and kids of our group. Dad exemplified calm and care. He was such a powerful example that to this day many of the "kids" from that trip still mention it to me.

One of the kids who went on multiple mission trips told him, "When I think of you, I think of your real big smile, your humor, your willingness to listen, and your miles and miles of patience... endless patience! You have made such a difference in so many lives just by being you, by being there to set a positive example."

I have so many great memories from youth group and our Kentucky trips, but it is Dad's example as a youth leader I draw from while I lead and parent youth. I try to have that patience (and wow, can that be hard, to have that patience sometimes! I have much more respect for my Dad now.); I try to listen to my kids and any of the youth-group kids, just like Dad does. When I drove for the local school district, I listened to the kids on the bus without judgment. And yes, sometimes I even borrowed some of his corny humor!

For the next two decades, Dad continued to show his love for others in the Appalachian Mountains of Eastern Kentucky and in many other locations across the U.S. To witness his caring nature against the backdrop of the beautiful Appalachians helped me realize God was working through my dad in so many ways, despite the extreme poverty! I count myself blessed to rely on God like Dad demonstrated on a daily basis. I pray I can be that example for someone else!

Dad, thank you for the impact you've made on my life and the lives of all of us. Sometimes the little things add up to greatness. I hope you know how much you are appreciated and loved. I hope you know you are great. It's not easy to have your kind of an impact without first fully relying on God!

The second person is Earl Madary, my youth-group director when I was a teenager. Sadly, Earl was taken from this world way too early. He, like my dad, epitomized what it means to fully rely on God.

One example that pops into my head is an experience Earl had when planning our second mission trip. He was in his office at church when he got a phone call informing him his father had just passed away.

After Earl hung up the phone, a homeless man came to the door, looking for money. Earl first told the man he didn't have any money on him; then remembered he had the funds from our mission trip. He got the money bag, took it to the gentleman and offered it to him. The man reached into the bag, took out $1.00 and said, "Your father is now in heaven," then walked away.

Earl was a beacon of peace and calm throughout the time I was blessed to have him in my life. He was always compassionate and wanted justice for everyone, which led him to help establish A Place of Grace Catholic Worker House in La Crosse, Wisconsin.

Last, I would like to talk about my Uncle Ken, another influential soul taken from us way too soon. He was one to never complain about having been a teenage diabetic, enduring the disease that eventually took his life. He always looked at the positive in his life. He knew he was going be gone early, so he tried to share with us kids all he knew about cars and life. Even though we were never able to discuss God in depth, I know he relied on God to get him through.

Uncle Ken often used humor to power through his days, which he passed on to his son. One day, shortly after Uncle Ken's lower leg was amputated, he and his nine-year-old son were watching TV in their living room and Ken wanted a drink. He turned to his son and asked him to get him a drink from the kitchen. Without missing a beat, his young son jokingly replied, "Get it yourself. You still have two arms, and a leg and a half." That was just the kick in the pants he needed to get up and get going – literally and figuratively.

If all of us can take something from these three men of God, our world would be much better off.

GRANDMA'S LOVE
Elizabeth Jeffords

Like many, I have been blessed to share this journey on earth with a number of men who have positively influenced my life. The list starts with Our Father, Christ, my dad, my grandfathers, my husband, my father-in-law, my uncles, my brother, priests, and youth directors, just to name a few. Nevertheless, as it nears Father's Day when I'm writing this, my grandma comes to mind when I think of my faith inspiration.

Grandma raised seven strong, loving, caring sons and one beautiful daughter. Grandpa passed at an early age, so it was up to Grandma to be both the father and the mother influence in raising her children. She was the grandfather and grandmother figure in the lives of all her grandchildren. Grandma rose to the task and, with God's help, excelled.

Through God's love, Grandma was able to live her life knowing God would help her through. Through her actions, she taught, her children and grandchildren that her love, as well as God's love, was unconditional. She also showed her children and grandchildren how to be caring, compassionate, kind, and generous. It was always a treat to visit Grandma, whether it was just for fun or if you had something you needed to talk about. Grandma would sit in her recliner and, without judgment, listen to anyone who needed an ear.

Grandma raised her children with God's love and full belief that God would take care of everything important. As I reflect upon her actions, I realize she had more faith than I could ever imagine. One example of her faith was in her patience. She knew someone would come to mow her lawn in the summer, even when the grass got a little longer than she liked. She never worried about how she was going to get to work after a snowfall because she raised her children to care for others and she knew one of them would make sure she got out.

Another example of Grandma's patience and faith was that she would make a meal every Sunday evening and then sit in her recliner, waiting for family to come to enjoy the fruits of her labor. She made no phone calls to ensure people were coming and never worried about the food getting cold. Instead, she just waited in faith.

Grandma shared her patience and peace with everyone who came through her door. And although she did not raise perfect children – and certainly did not expect perfect grandchildren – she loved everyone the same. She neither judged nor condemned the grandchildren who became parents before marriage; instead, she prayed for them and their children. Grandma did not criticize anyone for not following in her faith journey, but prayed for everyone.

Grandma lived by herself and never locked the doors to her house. She believed if someone came in and took something from her, they needed it more than she did. It probably doesn't even need to be said Grandma's house was never burglarized. The inspirational saying,

"Love them all and I'll sort them out later,"
fully describes the way my grandmother lived
her life – and the way God asks us to live our
earthly journeys.

When it came time for God to take
Grandma from this world, she went peacefully,
ready to answer to God for all she had done.
There was no doubt in Grandma's mind that
when she got to Heaven, God would take care
of her and would answer any questions she
had while on earth. I pray daily I will be able
to share with others just a mustard seed-sized
portion of the faith my grandma shared.

FROG TIME
Francis Jeffords

In my Irish stubbornness, I knew I was going to be a priest. God knew otherwise. *I* wanted to be a priest. But God had other plans.

"God, should I be a priest?" I asked.

God said, "No."

"But..."

Again, God said, "NO."

I eventually relented. "FINE." Such a Type-A response!

My spiritual life was pretty solid. With the church, sacraments, and my being an Irish Type-A sort, I felt my union with God was good. I knew what it meant to be Catholic. I had it going. During my time on this earth, I knew what I wanted and how to fit my idea into where I was going. Yeah, right.

Silly Irishman.

I joined the church choir and I taught sixth-grade religious-education classes. I wanted to teach those young minds all I knew about God. How little did I know! God made me aware of His presence one night after choir practice. As my wife, Connie, and I were walking down the stairs to go home, Earl, our choir director, called me back up to his apartment and handed me his phone. My son was on the line, informing me my brother Tom had died earlier that evening.

My legs became like rubber. I could not focus on my surroundings. I started down the stairs again, completely lost in my thoughts and grief. When I drove to Tom's funeral later that week, I still was kind of in a fog. While I tried to put on a brave face for Tom's wife and kids, I was hurting so bad. I looked at my mother and tried to be solid for her. One of her children had just died. I could not imagine what it was like to lose your child. God seemed to have retreated to the background in my life. I still believed in God, but not in the same way.

Two weeks after Tom's funeral, my sister-in-law Janice called late one night. Quietly, she told me my brother Ken was in trouble and asked me to please hurry over. When I walked in the back door, the medics were just putting Ken in the ambulance. I followed them to the hospital. Ken had suffered a heart attack. To me, God had again disappeared into the background.

Weeks down the road, I received another 3 a.m. call. Janice was crying into the phone. Ken had another heart attack. Please hurry.

Again, I reached the back door just as the EMTs were taking Ken down the front steps for another trip to the hospital. This time I rode in the ambulance with him. Our wives followed in the car. When Ken was wheeled into the ER, I knew this was not good.

The doctors and nurses left me alone with Ken. I talked to him like I did on the ambulance ride down. Ken was my fishing buddy (okay, maybe we were more like worm-drowning buddies). In the silence of the room after he died, I started praying in earnest, asking God to help him and his family in the days following.

The wake was hard – the hardest thing I

knew ever since my father's funeral years before. I was standing in the back of the room crying to myself when my older brother Mike came up to me. I always looked up to Mike because he was a Marine who had survived eighteen months in Vietnam. As I cried for Ken, Mike told me to stop. How could he say that? Later, I understood I needed to put my sorrow in *God's* hands. That day put me on a journey to understanding my faith more. For so many years I had thought I controlled my life.

I reflected on Ken's life. In earlier years, he had to have the lower part of his right leg amputated because of diabetes. Afterward, he fought to go back to work and succeeded with the addition of a new leg. He was surviving in life.

More health issues popped up for Ken. He began retaining water around his heart, which dragged his optimism down. He started dialysis. One night he called me around 3 a.m. because he did not want to wake his wife. Good, smart man. When we got settled in at the clinic, with Ken on the dialysis machine and me in a recliner in the waiting room, I tried to catch a few winks. Suddenly my cell phone rang, jolting me out of my sleep. I just knew the person on the phone had to be Ken.

I yanked the chair handle to bring the recliner to an upright position; it launched me across the carpet on my hands and knees. Stopping short of planting myself into the opposing wall, I answered the phone to hear my brother asking me to bring him a glass of water.

I told Ken, "No! This is why we are in the clinic so the machine can take the excess water out of your body. It would be counterproductive to give you water. Why don't you ask a nurse for some ice chips instead?!" He thought that idea would be better. Again, smart man. Good call.

In addition to the deaths of Ken and Tom, I would lose two sisters and my mom in less than seven years' time. Shortly after Ken's death, I still was helping with the church youth group. By getting involved with high school-age students' lives through regular meetings, lock-ins, and retreats, I found myself. This is when I realized God had been in my life all along. God had used these lows and highs to form a new me. Finally I was aware that God was really talking to ME. What a dead head I was!

This understanding came to me one night after many years of teaching young people how to relate to God. During a high-school retreat at church, we were training students for an upcoming mission trip. We were anticipating taking these students to work in the eastern hills of Kentucky. Kentucky had many of God's children: the poor coal miners and their families who were barely surviving in life. One of the students thought Kentucky was a Third World country. So many people had abused them over the years, keeping them isolated. They had come to just accept it; they figured no one cared for them. We wanted to help them and during the process, we could show young (and not-so-young) people what God had been telling me for so many years: We are to take care of His children in whatever way we could.

During this retreat, after sharing some of my life experiences, it was late at night and I walked out to an area where everyone was sleeping (or supposed to be sleeping). I was whistling under my breath when Angie, one of the student mission-team members, came up to me. She asked me how I could whistle, so carefree, when I had just buried my brother, my best friend, my worm-drowning buddy.

I answered her the only way I could. I told Angie God had shown me I could put my whole life in His hands. I did not have to worry. God was controlling my life. I reminded her of the parable when Jesus told His apostles to look at the birds of the air. They did not worry about where to get food, or how beautiful their feathers were. They were adorned with colors fit for a king. Jesus taught how lowly the birds were. If He would care for them, how much more would He care for us?

That little interaction with Angie, His child in this retreat, taught me how much God cares for me. This child taught me we as human beings have to stop trying to run or control our lives because God has us in His hands. We are protected every day of our lives. This means when we think there is no way out and we worry, stop. Just STOP. He will make sure we will be okay with Him. We are destined to be with God. We really are designed according to His plan, but God, in His great wisdom, lets us decide that on our own.

We make our own choices. God is with

Christina M. Eder

us but *we* have to make the move toward Him. I finally realized if we think God is not in our life, we feel He is just not there. You have to ask yourself, "Who moved?"

Next time you feel overwhelmed, out of control, or lost, just STOP! Choose God. Let Him take over your life. He does and always will. If you can just let it go, you will feel peace in ways you never thought were possible. When you feel distant from God, always ask yourself, "Who moved?"

Choose God. Choose God because He has already chosen you!

MY ORDINARY MOMENTS WITH GOD
Tom LaFleur

When my dad built our family home, he was not planning on a large family, but he included a 12x28 open attic that offered extra space if needed. The narrow steps going to the attic were steep, unfinished, and uneven. In the winter, ice would build up to a half inch on the windows upstairs and there was only one duct in the floor for heat. We would hurry downstairs each morning to eat breakfast near a heat register, fighting for the closest spots. Summers were as hot as winters were cold. I remember playing outside in winter and Mom would have to pry the frozen boots off our feet when we came indoors. To this day, I have frostbitten sensitive toes, fingers, ears and can only guess when that happened.

Dad was both harsh and fair. We had a simple rule: "Do as you're told, or else."

Mom was average, yet a saint with eight kids – seven of whom were boys. She could easily control all of us with one sentence: "Wait until your dad gets home!"

I was born in 1959, one of eight children. My six brothers were as different as night and day. My lone sister had the bedroom next to Mom and Dad's on the main floor. We all went to Catholic grade school and then had our choice for high school. Growing up with 10 of us in a two-bedroom, one-bathroom house, I had to learn trust and patience.

When I was 12 and in seventh grade, my father became disabled. We were forced to grow up a little faster. Dad needed help with daily things, like getting dressed, going to the bathroom, even walking to his chair. Dad was one of the first open-heart surgery patients in the country. He suffered a stroke during the operation and became paralyzed on his right side.

One day when I was 14, I was home sick, in that open dormer where all seven of us boys slept. Dad crawled up those narrow, uneven, unfinished stairs to bring me a glass of water and aspirin. I can only imagine how a person paralyzed on his right side could crawl to the kitchen, reach a glass out of an upper cabinet, fill it with water, crawl up a set of steep stairs, and then crawl back down those same steps. It must have been a long process, and I was too young and too sick to understand. That was the first time I recognized God working through people.

Since that early revelation, I started seeing God moments in my life. I learned to appreciate God's presence when I noticed how Dad's coworkers would show up every couple of weeks. They would leave an envelope with Mom – they'd taken up a collection after payday. Mom would cry after they left every time.

Two months after Dad died, I had stopped to get my oil changed and met a girl. One look into her eyes and I told the friend who was with me I just met the girl I would marry. I didn't even know her name. That was August 29, 1977. We married in September of 1980, and I am still married to Donna today.

At age 30, I'd worked my way up to foreman of a crew. One day my boss asked me to lie to a customer. I told him I couldn't do that, so he said I would be fired if I didn't lie. To make matters worse, it was my wife's birthday. Again I said no, and was promptly fired. Not knowing what to do, I quickly made two phone calls and received two job offers within an hour. I went to meet with both people and chose my new job with a $1 per hour raise. When I went home that night, I knew God had my back.

Another God moment happened when I was driving to an appointment, thirty-some years ago. I took a wrong turn and ended up on the interstate from Wisconsin to Minnesota. Realizing my mistake, I called the customer to say I would be late. Being frazzled, I was not paying attention to where I was and ended up in the parking lot of a nursing home. Trying to clear my head, it dawned on me Charlie Drake, an older friend, was in that nursing home. Maybe I should stop in and say hi. As I went to the front desk to get his room number, I was told he was close to death. I now realized I must have been summoned to cheer him up, since he had no children and his wife had died years earlier.

When I walked into the room, Charlie was lying in bed, watching the door; when he saw me, his face lit up like a Christmas tree. He was thrilled to have company! We started talking about death; he believed in reincarnation. In an effort to change the topic, I brought up fishing. We were always going to get out to fish "someday." He always said he would land the big fish that would not get away. Charlie agreed we would fish someday, just not in the way we expected. Parting ways that day, I felt grateful for a wrong turn I had thought was a mistake.

Next morning, I learned Charlie died less than an hour after my visit – and I had been his only visitor in weeks. On my very next fishing outing, I landed a 20-pound northern pike without a fight. To this day, I've never landed a fish even close to that size!

Five years after what I thought was a wrong turn at the nursing home, I was driving to another appointment. Again, I made one wrong turn, followed by another. Frustrated, I pulled into the closest parking lot and saw my cousin Larry. I stopped to ask what he was up to, and he told me his dad was dying, then asked if I could stop to console his mother.

Larry was a wreck and admitted his emotional state was upsetting my aunt. Walking in the door, I saw my aunt crying and she told me my uncle was comatose. She was grateful I came by and talked me into going in to see him. Upon my holding his hand, my uncle looked up at me with the clearest blue eyes with a look that said he was ready to go. I called my aunt into the room, where we both said goodbye, and watched him die.

I write these little stories in the hope you can feel God in the simple relationships of life. God knows I'm not a person of accomplishment or great social stature, but I feel my life is blessed in ways beyond my understanding.

Is it possible for all these experiences to be accidents, or was God guiding me? A chance hello or a wrong turn and life will change. As a kid, I hated hospitals and chose not to see my father on his last day on earth. I eventually regretted that decision, but God has now given me a chance with this writing and these thoughts to make peace with that decision.

NEVER FEAR, I AM HERE
Irene Seng

I am amazed how often the Holy Spirit seems to be directing me through a project, even though I had no idea He was helping me until the project was completed.

One example of this was last winter, when I returned home from Orchard Manor Nursing Home in Lancaster, Wisconsin, after recovering from a broken hip and wrist. At that time, I realized I needed help with my cleaning. Fortunately, I found Heather, a teen-age girl in my neighborhood, who was interested in the job. After a couple of visits, she asked me about my two sewing machines, one of which is a serger. Since that was a totally new machine to her, I gave her a quick demonstration on how it works.

Later Heather asked, "Would you help me make a dress?"

A red flag came up and I hesitated, because three times prior to this, I had decided to give up doing alterations for people and then changed my mind.

Then I thought, "Why not? I enjoy sewing and will have plenty of time, since it is winter and I will be staying home more." It was as if the Holy Spirit was telling me that, at the age of 91, I could still be useful to someone who wanted to learn about a talent I have.

I asked, "Do you have a pattern?"

She replied, "No, but I have material."

Although Heather wished to sew a dress, I thought making a quilt would be an easier project for a beginner. Again, the Holy Spirit was with me, and I recalled one of my nieces works at Land's End, a factory that sells all types of clothing. Employees are allowed to take fabric from a designated receptacle if they wish to use it. I asked her if the next time she got fabric she'd save some for me. A couple of weeks later, I looked through three boxes of a variety of fabrics and picked out four different pastels, which I cut into six-inch squares for my neighbor girl to practice sewing straight lines.

The next visit, after Heather finished her cleaning, we started on the project. She started sewing the squares, which made a diagonal design; she finished within a couple of visits.

When the quilt top was completed, we pinned it to the backing, which also was part of the free fabric. Next she made the binding and secured the front and back together while sewing on the binding. When she came to a corner, I taught her how to make a mitered corner. She finished the project by hand-stitching the binding to the back fabric. It was obvious she was proud of her project. I was amazed at her interest and patience and was happy to see what she had accomplished. Later I learned she showed the quilt to a couple other people.

Most of the sewing was done on my machine, as Heather's mother's machine needed repair. Her mother was able to buy a sewing machine from another niece of mine who has a collection of used ones and had two similar sewing machines to choose from. Now we are calling on the Holy Spirit as to where we can get this machine tuned up for future projects.

I don't know whether Heather still wants to make a dress, because she also talked about the possibility of making a shirt. Two of her challenges include the high cost of purchasing a pattern and fabric.

Now that it is spring, my young neighbor is more interested in being outdoors with her horse; however, I am sure she will get back to sewing. Meanwhile, she is still helping me clean. Isn't it interesting how the Holy Spirit brought the both of us together to assist each other? Thank you, Holy Spirit, for this situation and the many other ways you have provided for me in the past!

MY LIFE PATH WITH GOD
John Williams

It has taken me much time to title this story and reflect on how I have gotten to this point in life. Now I realize it isn't difficult to see who was really responsible for where I am. God has been with me the entire time. In looking back, I see who I am and why I experienced so many disappointments.

My parents are responsible for opening my eyes to God, from our time in church to the way they lived. My biggest problem was that I had no self-confidence. I had a big issue with the way I felt people thought of me. I had a couple of friends, but for the most part, they didn't have much to do with me. I stood out as a perfect bully target. My inability to stand up for myself weighed heavy on me. Still, I had this feeling Someone was watching over me and caring for me.

I depended a lot on my parents and my siblings for social upbringing. Church was important and I always felt good about being there. I've always regretted not being an altar server, but the timing never seemed to work out. I felt right at home with the nuns, who were very influential. I was told I would make a good priest, but as time went on, the idea of being ordained never lasted.

I wasn't sure what to do after high school. I have always had a problem with reading and comprehension. My inability to read as strongly or easily comprehend like my classmates felt like what I imagine a crown of thorns over my head would be like.

My family was military strong. My dad and four brothers joined various branches of the military. One brother fought in both the Korean and Vietnam wars. Another brother battled in Vietnam, so I joined the Army, thinking I wanted to go to Vietnam; instead, I was sent to Germany. I look back and believe I did not have it in me to be a combat soldier who would come home in one piece. There again, God was directing me. I spent my entire time with the Construction Engineers.

During this time, my self-esteem dipped, leaving my soul feeling battered. At the same time, in the early '70s, our country faced a multitude of challenging social issues.

Once I returned home from the service, I went through a great deal of career and soul searching. I had had a dream of being a police officer, so after trying several different jobs, I went to the police academy. That was difficult because of my reading issues, but I made it through and secured a job with the La Crosse Police Department. I spent eleven months trying to prove I was mentally tough enough for this career. That left a big question between God and me: What should I do? The best answer that came out of this question was in my meeting Kim, a dispatcher at the police department at that time.

I decided to go rejoin the military and go back to construction. Kim and I got married and we went to Ft. Lewis, Washington, for thirteen months, where our daughter Meredith was born. I felt so blessed with a new wife and child, but Kim would say it was just the beginning of our not-so-boring life together. We had little money, but made the best of it. I was back to spending Sundays in church and time with family.

Remember I said "not-so-boring life"? We had Meredith baptized May 17 and the next day, Mount St. Helen's erupted. We could see the volcano from our living-room window.

I received orders to go to an isolated post in Alaska. I sent Kim and Meredith home and went to Ft. Greeley for a year. When I received my next orders for Ft. Belvoir, Virginia, I packed up my family and off we went for two years. During that time, our son Matthew was born.

The not-so-boring life? Washington had the worst snowstorm in its history that year; it was also the winter a passenger plane hit the 14th Street Bridge and went into the Potomac River, killing all but four people on board. My troop was on standby to recover survivors, but I didn't have to go. My time at Ft. Belvoir was ending, but the Army was unwilling to offer me a duty station I wanted in order to re-enlist.

This was the first time I trusted God to this degree. With my wife and two children, I packed up everything and went home to Wisconsin. Before I left the military, I signed up with the National Guard unit in Onalaska, Wisconsin. Trusting the direction in which God was leading me became more important. I didn't figure I was ever going to have a lot of money, but it didn't matter.

I was offered a maintenance job at a clinic and assigned to the supply area. I spent twelve wonderful years at the clinic and learned about building maintenance, supply work, and people. I learned how to listen to people and made great friends.

We started getting involved with St. Patrick's Church in Onalaska. I joined the choir and volunteered in the building and grounds area. In 1994, our deacon and pastor called to offer me a job as the head of buildings and grounds for the parish. I couldn't say yes fast enough. Funny thing is, some people think they could slide onto Easy Street with a job like this. As our current pastor would say, "Wrong!"

After a few years of work, choir, and social-justice projects, I let things go to my head. I was trying so hard to make things happen, trusting the wrong people, and making some bad choices. Like St. Paul, I got knocked off my horse and was brought down to earth. I lost my position with the church and school and, as a result, I felt like I had let everyone down.

During that time, Kim had a spiritual awakening. She took a trip with her grandma to see Mother Angelica. Kim had gone along just to help her grandma, but came away with a life-changing experience. She ended up going to confession, receiving Communion, and coming home with a new outlook. Daily, I see her growing.

After leaving my employment with the church, I fell into a deep depression. I asked myself, "How could I allow this to happen?" I questioned my faith but was slowly climbing back up out of my depression when I took a job at a lumber yard and then at the local university as a custodian. My son enlisted in the Army and ended up going to Iraq.

When Matthew went to war, I leaned on God more than ever. Every morning for ten months, I turned on the news to find out if anyone died. Once I knew everyone was okay, I could go to work for another day. I started getting my head on straight. My faith and my prayer life were coming back stronger.

I was thankful God brought my son home, not knowing Matthew was having problems. The Army had "stop lost" him from getting out of the service and sent him back to Iraq for another year. (Editor's note: stop lost means to retain members of the armed forces on active duty beyond their originally agreed period of enlistment). He started over again and we were able to welcome him home a second time a year later.

I took another job at the care center where my mother was a resident. Mom had dementia, so this job gave me a chance to be with her. I got to take care of Mom and got the reward of meeting other patients. On April 8, 2008, Mom went home to God and emotionally I couldn't work at the care center anymore.

About that time, a security job opened up at the county courthouse and, because I had law-enforcement experience, I got the job. My life was getting back on track, but I had no idea that I had much more to look forward to.

I also joined the Knights of Columbus. During the knighting ceremony, I felt peace and strength come over me. I felt a growing need to become active with the church and school again. When I was 62, I was struck with an epiphany of what to do with the rest of my life: I 'd use my construction-engineering background to literally help build the family of God.

With my military and state benefits in place, I could retire. I went to our deacon, who said he could keep me as busy as I wanted to be. I volunteered with church, school, choir, and social-justice committee.

A fabulous thing has happened since I retired. I stopped taking things so personally. Word got out I was available to help others with their home repairs. I recognize what some people in churches can be like, but I don't let them get under my skin or drag me down anymore. I find joy in helping at school. I'm most grateful for the trust our deacon, pastor, and school principal have in me.

I have come to this part of my life and look back on everything, knowing now why some things worked and others did not. All I want to do with the rest of my life is pay it forward and serve God in any way I can. I need to follow His direction and pray I can do this for many years.

REINTEGRATION
Matthew Williams

While serving my second tour in Iraq, I became a sergeant and was in charge of a three-truck convoy for my Brigade Commander. This involved being his Personal Security Detachment (PSD), which is kind of like what the Secret Service does for the president.

Our Infantry Brigade Commander never sat behind a desk, so as infantrymen, my team and I were never bored. I believe we conducted more than 555 missions in one year, which included raids, surveillance, transport and humanitarian aid.

During that tour, my eyes and heart really opened. Some of my friends were also on their second tours of being away from their wives and children. I realized I never wanted to do that to my future family. I also learned I never will take anything for granted, good or bad. I'll always be thankful for what I have.

I was skilled at what I did in the Army, or so I thought. In less than three years' time, I became a sergeant and had a chance to go Special Forces school and Sniper school. That included a tax-free re-enlistment bonus of $24,500 if I signed up for two more years. As I was preparing for a mission one day, I realized if I was going to go Special Forces (my dream at the time), I needed to commit myself one hundred percent.

During that moment, it's almost like I heard a voice calling me home. I thought about my dad and how much I missed him. I thought of all the time I had lost with him and how much he could teach me on being a future dad, homeowner and husband.

I also thought of all the men we'd lost, the "too many close calls" I've had and wondered (to this day) why wasn't that me? At that realization point, I declined the offer to re-enlist.

After my honorable discharge from the Army, I enrolled in school and became a police officer. I had a difficult time transitioning back into civilian life. My enlistment was for three years, but I was stopped lost, which meant I couldn't get out when I was supposed to. I ended up spending 32 months in Iraq. I was part of the initial invasion in 2003 and spent from the end of 2004 to the beginning of 2006 in Sadir City, Iraq.

(On a side note, while I was in school, my parents had known something was up with me. Long story short, they gave me the best counselor/psychologist anyone could ask for. A yellow Lab, whom I named Snoop. He listened to me and never judged. To this day I owe my life to Snoop.)

After graduating with a degree in criminal justice, I became a police officer for a small village in Wisconsin and then became deputy sheriff. It wasn't until I met my future wife, who lived two hours away, that I decided to make a change. After working all night, I would drive two hours to spend a half a day with her, and then drive back to work.

I thought about how my friends and their families struggled, being so far away in the Army and realized I didn't want to be away from her. I left my sheriff's deputy job and had dreams of becoming a detective. But I loved her more and didn't want to be away. In 2012 we married.

In 2012, before we married, I graduated with my bachelor's degree and went back into police work. In 2014, our first child was born; since then, I can't stand being away from him. In 2018, we had our second child.

I've had chances to return to the type of "regular" police work you might see on TV, but something was holding me back. I don't do high-speed chases anymore. I don't kick in doors. I don't "run and gun" anymore and the big thing is I don't work nights, so I'm always home at night for my family.

Since 2012, I've been a police officer for the U.S. Department of Veterans Affairs. VAPD officers are sworn law-enforcement officers, but our main purpose is to treat and care for veterans. Although we make arrests and conduct investigations into veterans and Veterans Affairs employees, our first mission is to care for veterans. We're a different type of police.

What I do now is help fellow veterans, which is a kind of assistance I never had when I got out. When I was discharged, no one told me to go to the VA or seek help if I felt suicidal, couldn't sleep, or had anxiety. I struggled with reintegrating into society. I was simply told to take my discharge paper to my county service office and go to school.

Besides upholding the law, I educate veterans of all ages to get the help they need, whether it's mental health, substance-abuse help, job assistance, or education information. Do I miss the "run and gun" type of police work? Occasionally, but I'm glad I'm home at night with my family.

Since I had children, I look at life differently. I grew up and take nothing for granted. I love being married. I have the best wife and mother to my children a guy could ask for. With the help and love from my dad, I've been successful at being a husband and a father.

I feel that on that day in Iraq, I heard the Lord calling me home. My mission in Iraq and ridding that country of an evil dictator was over. My new mission in life is being a loving husband, amazing father and facilitator to veterans. Do I arrest veterans? Yes, but that is my last resort.

Since my marriage and becoming a homeowner, my dad has been there right from the start. He teaches me about house care, rebuilding, and upkeep of a home. He's also taught me about patience and keeping the Lord close to my heart. The only way I can repay Dad is by doing the Lord's work and teaching my kids what he's taught me.

In the Army's Third Infantry Division 2nd Brigade Combat Team, there is quote that says, "Send me." From Isaiah 6:8, "I heard the voice of the Lord saying, 'Whom shall I send? And who will go for us?' And I said, 'Here am I. Send me!'" I heard the voice in 2002 and fought for people who couldn't stand up and fight back. I heard that same voice, the voice of the Lord, sending me home to keep our streets safe, to serve and educate fellow veterans, and to be the best mentor, father, and husband I can be.

I had thought seeing the smiling faces of Iraqi children and helping some of the poorest people on Earth would be the best thing, but being a dad and husband is the best thing that has happened to me. I'm grateful I heard – and heeded – the voice of the Lord calling me home.

Christina M. Eder

AUTHOR BIOS

Mary Ballinger lives in Onalaska, Wisconsin, with her husband, Tom. She enjoyed many years raising their four children and now teaches other children at a local daycare. Her grandchildren, gardening, and volunteering at church fill her extra time.

Born and raised in Wisconsin, Tom Ballinger enjoys many outdoor activities in the North Country, including deer hunting and Muskie fishing. God, his wife, Mary, four children and three grandchildren remain the focus of his life.

Brenda Brandt is a retired teacher and former director of the Family Resource Center in La Crosse, Wisconsin. She is the proud mother of three daughters and four grandchildren. Her hobbies include spending time with family and friends, hosting bonfires, learning about her faith, traveling, and helping provide faith-filled programs at her parish. Little did she know when she met Christina they would share many years of friendship and this "frozen" FROG experience!

Todd Eder is father to three spirited daughters, and husband to his beautiful wife, Candice. He works as an unexploded-ordnance technician across the country. When he's not traveling for his job, Todd lives in Kentucky and loves spending time with his family. His hobbies include hiking, fishing, concerts, playing the guitar, and following Milwaukee Brewers and Green Bay Packers games.

Elizabeth Demos Garibaldi is a disciple of the Lord Jesus under the Mantle of the Blessed Mother. She is the mother of one daughter on earth, one child in heaven, and a spiritual mother to many. Elizabeth came into her faith later in life and is now passionately pursuing the call to holiness through prayer, the Sacraments of the Catholic Church, works of mercy, and pointing the way for others to have a personal relationship with Christ. Heaven is her goal. Our lives are History.

Brian Jeffords is a husband and father living in frozen western Wisconsin. In his free time, he enjoys watching his children participate in their activities. He loves working on vehicles in the garage with his wife and kids.

Elizabeth Jeffords is a wife and mother of two, living in Wisconsin. She enjoys reading and is honored to be able to share her story in this inspirational book. When not working or reading, she is the taxi driver, cheerleader, and biggest fan for her kids' activities.

Francis Jeffords was born in Milwaukee, Wisconsin, during the Korean War. When his dad died in 1965, their family moved to Cashton, Wisconsin, population 728. A big-city kid in a little town, Frank became involved with youth ministry in 1987 and continues investing in youth. He and his wife, Connie, have one son, a daughter-in-law, and two grandchildren, all living in Onalaska, Wisconsin, population 18,712.

Tom LaFleur grew up in LaCrosse, Wisconsin, across the Mississippi River from LaCrescent, Minnesota. He and his wife, Donna, have been married 39 years and have three children, three in-laws, and five grandchildren. When not working at his self-employed construction business, Tom loves to be out fishing and hunting. He said, 'I always have and always will hunt and fish, even though some days my legs tell me otherwise."

Irene Seng is a proud mother to four children, 12 grandchildren and nine great-grandchildren, as well as 10 dogs. After retiring from farming with her husband in southwestern Wisconsin, she enjoyed bowling and playing cards. Her hobbies currently include helping those in need, texting the grandchildren, sewing for family, and doing alterations for others.

John Williams was born and raised in the La Crosse-Onalaska, Wisconsin, area. He comes from a Christian home and is the youngest of nine children. He served seven years in the Army and thirteen years in the National Guard, from which he retired. He is married to his wonderful wife, Kim; they have two children and four grandchildren. John credits a great family and church that mean everything to his family and him.

Matt Williams grew up in Onalaska, Wisconsin. After high school, he joined the Army for three years and was honorably discharged in 2006. In 2009, he became a police officer and a deputy sheriff and moved to Madison, Wisconsin, where he graduated with his bachelor's degree and met his future wife. Matt and his wife are married with two children. Aside from his favorite roles as husband and father, Matt enjoys sports, fishing, and hunting.

AUTHOR Q & A

Q: Is this *FROG Blog* collection kind of like the *Chicken Soup for the Soul* books?

A: Not exactly. I choose to think of them as frog legs for the spirit.

Q: How do you develop your insights?

A: Every day I live as a curiously awkward seventh grader searching for direction, understanding, and acceptance. And after almost 50 revolutions around the sun, I'm still that seventh grader, only now I've added 38 years' additional experience to draw upon.

Q: Where do you come up with your ideas?

A: The short answer is I frequent airports and simply listen and observe. Authors aren't typically in the highest-paid career lists, so I supplement my income by having people pay me to stay *out* of my books! Okay, you have to promise you'll put that last part in a sarcastic font when you publish this.

Q: What are the best compliments you've received as a writer?

A: I remember the unique ones most. A lady once said, "I loved your first book so much that

I had to loan it to my mother-in-law. It's been one of the few friendly exchanges we've made in years." I also liked when someone told me he got two copies so he could lend one and keep the one he'd highlighted. To me, a book is noteworthy when I grab a highlighter for future reference.

Q: When you first published your books, what surprised you most?

A: I didn't realize I would have to expand my social circle. As an introvert who requires much space and quiet time, I used to define a "convention" as having more than four people at one function. Before publishing, I hadn't factored social media, author events, bookstore and library engagements, or public-speaking requests into my equation. I still value the six closest people in my inner circle. Of course, not all six of them at once!

THANK YOU FROM CHRISTINA

Thank you to my two main editors, Dave Dutrow and Rita M. Reali. Dave blended his engineering mind, spiritual compass, and comical approach to editing with an animated medley. Dave "strongly encouraged" me to get my first book into print after he had his book, *Caution Ahead: 94 Ways to Navigate Parenting*, published. Rita, an author and blogger in her own right, willingly crossed time zones and broke my inner social sound barriers to teach my literary voice how to speak. I encourage you to read her fiction (available from your favorite online bookseller) and her editing advice at persnicketyproofreader.wordpress.com.

Thank you to my cover designer, Red Paint Spilman, who designed the first of what's destined to be a five-book series in the *FROG Blog* collection. I'm grateful that with Red Paint's theatre experience, he understands directing multiple pieces of a production can be a series of dress rehearsals. His gracious flexibility showed me what it meant to bend a knee without breaking a leg.

To you, my reader. Amid the world's well-supplied bookshelves, I truly appreciate your investing your time and resources to read my books. I love hearing from readers, especially when they handwrite notes and cards. If any part of this book has inspired or invited you to think in a new way, please drop me a line or write an online review. The online review may be to simply copy the book quote that moved you most and what made it stand out.

If there is a chapter or topic that has intrigued you, I can tailor a workshop or be a speaker for your group event. And if you want to contact a specific author from the FROG anthology series, please contact me and I'll act as the bridge to connect reader and writer.

Christina M. Eder
P.O. Box 5181
Oak Ridge, TN 37830
www.gueststarcoaching.com

Leaping off the lily pad to write color into the world,

Christina

CPSIA information can be obtained
at www.ICGtesting.com
Printed in the USA
LVHW081741020820
662196LV00019B/2240

9 781734 659603